MW00531869

ESCAPE
THE
WLF

ESCAPE
THE
W🎯LF

A Seal Operative's Guide To
Situational Awareness, Threat Identification,
And Getting Off The X

CLINTON EMERSON

LIONCREST

COPYRIGHT © 2022 CLINT EMERSON

All rights reserved.

ESCAPE THE WOLF

A SEAL Operative's Guide To Situational Awareness, Threat Identification, And Getting Off The X

ISBN   978-1-5445-2995-0   *Paperback*

        978-1-5445-2996-7   *Ebook*

CONTENTS

PREFACE

WHY DO SOME TRAVELERS SEEM TO INVITE CRIME?

What steps can you take to make yourself less vulnerable?

How can you minimize exposure to illness, natural disasters, and other threats when traveling?

This book will show you how to avoid being a "walking target" and provide a holistic approach to avoiding and minimizing threats while traveling.

Awareness is the key.

* * *

You know that feeling when you're at the beach and you're swimming in the ocean, and you get that eerie, creepy sense that there's a shark nearby? That's because there probably is. Our bodies are attuned to danger. When you visit an unfamiliar place, and you feel uneasy, pay attention. There may be a good reason you're feeling that way.

Escape the Wolf's goal is to prepare the global traveler to cope with the unexpected. The lessons shared in this book can help put you at ease and keep you safe, whether you are traveling around the globe or around the corner. I speak from experience, for each and every one of the scenarios I describe here has happened to me. Are they all likely to happen to you? Probably not, but travel security is about being ready for anything. Because if something *does* happen while you are traveling internationally, the stakes are high, and you have fewer resources to draw upon.

What if your wallet gets lifted? What if you are the victim of a carjacking or hotel intrusion? What if you become ill or are in the aftermath of a hurricane or earthquake? What if you are thrown in jail in a foreign country because of a misunderstanding? What if you are kidnapped? Each of these scenarios has a varying degree of likelihood. But an understanding of travel security is like a life insurance policy. Why not proceed with a good, solid plan?

That plan begins and ends with awareness training. Awareness training is something that I, and other folks who travel to high-risk areas during the course of our daily jobs, have drawn upon to avoid and minimize trouble. Basic awareness training is useful not only as a risk mitigation tool but also as a valuable form of cultural currency. Because awareness training can make it possible for travelers to forge relationships with individuals in the local culture, it has the potential to make any business traveler's stay more pleasant and smooth—and ultimately more successful.

Be aware. Stay safe.

INTRODUCTION

SHEEP, WOLVES, AND SHEEPDOGS— *WHICH ONE ARE YOU?*

A DARK AND FOREBODING CREATURE FOUND THROUGHOUT THE AGES IN fairy tales from "Little Red Riding Hood" to Russia's "Peter and the Wolf," the wolf is a near-universal symbol for a predator. In these and other cautionary tales, the dangers that lurk just beyond the safety of the familiar village are embodied in the form of the wild and restless animal.

Escape the Wolf takes its title from this symbol, but more specifically from the imagery evoked by Lt. Col. Dave Grossman, who has spoken so eloquently about the root causes of the current wave of violent crime that threatens the world. A former West Point psychology professor, professor of military science, and Army Ranger, Grossman is one of the world's foremost experts in the field of human aggression and the roots of violence and violent crime. In *On Combat: The Psychology and Physiology of Deadly Conflict, In War and In Peace*, he paints a vivid picture of awareness and gives us language that helps us define the threats average citizens face:

> Most of the people in our society are sheep. They are kind, gentle, productive creatures who can only hurt one another by accident. This is true. Remember, the murder rate is six per 100,000 per year, and the aggravated assault rate is four per 1,000 per year. What this means is that the vast majority of Americans are not inclined to hurt one another. Some estimates say that two million Americans are victims of violent crimes every year, a tragic, stagger- ing number, perhaps an all-time record rate of violent crime. But there are almost 300 million Americans, which means that the odds of being a victim of violent crime is considerably less than one in a hundred in any given year. Furthermore, since many violent crimes are committed by repeat offenders, the actual number of violent citizens is considerably less than two million.

> Thus there is a paradox, and we must grasp both ends of the situation: We may well be in the most violent times in history, but violence is still remarkably rare. This is because most citizens are kind, decent people who are not capable of hurting each other, except by accident or under extreme provocation. They are sheep.

I mean nothing negative by calling them sheep. To me it is like the pretty, blue robin's egg. Inside it is soft and gooey but someday it will grow into something wonderful. But the egg cannot survive without its hard blue shell. Police officers, soldiers, and other warriors are like that shell, and someday the civilization they protect will grow into something wonderful. For now, though, they need warriors to protect them from the predators.

These predators are "the wolves," and the wolves feed on the sheep without mercy. Do you believe there are wolves out there who will feed on the flock without mercy? You better believe it. There are evil men in this world and they are capable of evil deeds. The moment you forget that or pretend it is not so, you become a sheep. There is no safety in denial.

The warriors are "sheepdogs"...and I'm a sheepdog. I live to protect the flock and confront the wolf. If you have no capacity for violence then you are a healthy productive citizen, a sheep. If you have a capacity for violence and no empathy for your fellow citizens, then you have defined an aggressive sociopath, a wolf. But what if you have a capacity for violence and a deep love for your fellow citizens? What do you have then? A sheepdog, a warrior, someone who is walking the hero's path. Someone who can walk into the heart of darkness, into the universal human phobia, and walk out unscathed.

Let's look at the sheep, sheepdog, and wolf as they relate to awareness. Sheep go about their business with their heads down and do not really worry about their surroundings. Sheep have a predictable daily schedule or routine and never step outside their comfort zone. As Grossman said, this is a perfectly fine way to live. But it means that sheep are easily targeted by wolves because of their complete lack of attention and awareness, especially of the environment around them. Another vocabulary note: When sheep die at the fangs of a wolf, they are called victims.

Grossman's sheepdog is a whole different animal. He is always aware. His ears are up; his nose is sensitive to the winds. His posture is alert and ready. Sheepdogs present themselves as dominant and intimidating to better manage the flock, but also to ward off potential threats. A sheepdog will engage in battle with the proper amount of force to neutralize the enemy, and to kill if necessary. When sheepdogs die at the fangs of a wolf, they are called heroes.

The evil wolf isn't necessarily a person—for us, the wolf represents all kinds of possible threats. Wolves are health threats, environmental threats, raids or attacks, technological threats—but, of course, they can also be terrorists. Wolves run in packs. Where there is one, there are many. The minute you engage just one, you will find yourself surrounded. Human wolves tend to attack when environmental ones have rendered the sheep vulnerable. And when wolves die at the fangs of a sheepdog, they are just dead, bad guys.

I invite you to embrace Grossman's mindset and to keep my definitions of the sheep, sheepdog, and wolf in mind. These terms will be helpful shorthand as we explore the concept of awareness more fully.

Sheep   **Sheepdog**   **Wolf**

THE TOTAL AWARENESS SYSTEM

IT'S 2010, AND I'M IN THE MIDDLE EAST. I HAD JUST LEFT THE EMBASSY in that country (can't get more specific than that, sorry), having picked up my usual gear from them—a local cell phone, an initial wad of cash, an embassy ID, and a gun. In this case, all I got was this tiny handgun.

I get in my car, drive a little bit, hang a right—and *damn*. Without warning, I'm surrounded by a thousand really angry people. And once they get a look at me and realize it's a white person in this car? Things get real scary real fast.

I grab for the phone the embassy gave me, and get this—it's not charged, and it doesn't even have a sim card yet. Useless. I eye my embassy ID, but I'm not sure that it'll help. It would absolutely identify me as an American, and these protesters aren't exactly pro-America. That badge would likely only make things worse.

Not that things can *get* much worse. The crowd is pressing in and shaking the car so violently my passenger and driver wheels are coming off the ground. I consider just flooring it and plowing through, but moving from a stop will mean that as soon as I run over about five people, the car will give up and my wheels will just be spinning—and then I'll have *really* pissed them off.

I've got a Sig 228 with two full mags, sixteen rounds per. If I pull that, I'm dead. Even if I manage to make every single shot count, there's way more than thirty-two people out there.

I'm stuck. People are yelling and screaming right at my face in the window, trying to get in. Eventually, they'll break the glass, and they'll pull me out of my car and rip me apart.

PRACTICAL EXAMPLE—WHAT WOULD YOU DO?

At this point, most people would panic. This is one of the scariest situations I've ever been in. Jumping out of an airplane? That's easy. Being caught unprepared in a situation you didn't anticipate? That's terrifying.

But there's a break in the crowd, a little place of calm, like a buoy in a sea of people. It's some sort of soldier or a member of local enforcement. He's holding an AK-47, but he doesn't look particularly angry. We make eye contact, and his eyes are sympathetic.

And there it is—my way out.

I raise my hand and quickly put up the international gesture for money, rubbing my thumb and forefinger together. I point at him, and rub my fingers again. The message is clear: "Wanna help me? I'll pay." He unslings his weapon and makes his way to my passenger door. He turns to face the crowd, and points his AK-47 at them. They all spread, creating enough of a bubble that he can open the door. I unlock the car and he climbs in.

We don't share a language, but we understand each other. I point at my windshield, and he aims the gun out the front. It's as if he's parting the sea, as everyone immediately runs to get out of the line of fire. I floor it. Once I get up to twenty or thirty miles per hour, I calm down—because now, if anyone jumps in front of my car, I'll just roll over them. I want to get perpendicular to the protest, so I make a left as soon as I can and drive several blocks away from the protest. We end up at a gas station. I give the guy a healthy chunk of cash, and he goes on his merry way.

I take a moment to gather myself. I mean, I just arrived in the country—I guess this is going to be quite a trip. I can hear birds chirping, and people going about their business at the gas pumps. It's completely calm, with absolutely no indication that several blocks away it's utter chaos.

It doesn't matter where you are on this planet. You can take a right-hand turn and all of a sudden you're in a holy mess. Think this scenario could only be found in a movie? Think again. This happened to *me*.

Global travelers face many dangers. Recognizing and preparing for them makes all the difference. Since that day, I've obviously always made sure my goddamn phone is charged and actually functional. But I survived thanks to extensive preparation and keeping calm. I made the right decision in the moment without having to go through lengthy and potentially dangerous deliberations. In the following chapters, we'll explore Escape the Wolf's Total Awareness® System. This proven approach prepares travelers for the unexpected, whether it's random crimes like pickpocketing and carjacking, or more serious issues like kidnapping.

"The real voyage of discovery consists not in seeking new landscapes but in having new eyes."

—MARCEL PROUST

BUILDING THE SKILL OF AWARENESS

One survival threat we seldom consider: modernity. Our basic human survival skills are being lost, replaced by technology and obscured by the busyness of everyday life. In general, people do not pay attention to their surroundings. When crisis strikes, they mentally stall and fall victim to preventable demise. People don't pull their heads out of their phones or laptops long enough to notice the clues that signal danger. We are losing our ability to be aware.

Some equate awareness to a sixth sense. Men call it instinct. Women call it intuition. Either way, it is one important way that we detect threats. It's powered by emotion and the subconscious, and is only rarely interpreted by the brain. That said, some people seem to have unusually good "spidey senses," better than most people. So as part of the research for this book, I conducted a brief survey of individuals in different occupations where awareness is instrumental to successful outcomes. The survey included fighter pilots, law enforcement SWAT officers, FBI agents, CIA clandestine operatives, special operation military operators, surgeons, and others. I asked, "Do you believe some people are born with a heightened sense of awareness?" The overwhelming answer was yes.

The next question in the survey was "Do you believe awareness can be taught?" Again, the overwhelming answer was

7

yes. These experienced, educated professionals agreed that some people are born with a heightened sense of awareness, but that awareness can be taught. And that's what we're doing right now—working to help you become more aware.

The thing is, though, awareness is contextual. That surgeon I talked to is amazing at monitoring a patient's vital signs and interpreting clues to figure out how to help them. But he's probably not so good at paying attention to his surroundings—and interpreting situations correctly—when he's just trying to relax on vacation.

Even if you have great instincts, how good are those instincts going to be in an unfamiliar environment? When traveling, our instincts are often either turned off, or they're hypercharged, firing off false alarms.

Remember that Halloween when you dressed as your favorite superhero and waited in line for the haunted house? You stood listening to the screams and let your anticipation build. When you finally got in, you were watching at every corner, listening to every sound, and trying so hard to spot the jump scare before it happened. But it never worked. Every time you thought something would happen—nothing. But the next moment, a mummy was scaring you out of your skin. Stepping foot into another country can be the same. Your instincts tell you one thing, but the results are entirely different. Eventually all those false alarms tell your brain to just relax and desensitize your instincts—which is when you become vulnerable to surprise or attack. The Total Awareness System will keep your guard up when your natural defense systems are down.

One of those surveyed made an interesting point. He agreed that awareness skills could be taught, but questioned whether *anyone* could make the right decisions, under stress, after potentially dangerous clues are recognized. Interesting point.

Connecting the dots and reacting in an effective manner takes education, experience, and practice. Instinct isn't enough—you have to *interpret* that instinct and make a smart decision, and you have to do it fast. To constantly be aware of surroundings and make effective decisions based on clues and cues requires a change of lifestyle. The Total Awareness approach is a lifestyle. Like any skill, it takes practice. You need to do it all the time to be good at it. If it is not a life-style, failure increases exponentially, especially in danger-ous environments.

Awareness is a weapon. If used properly, it can conceal your movements, ward off potential threats, prevent attacks, and ultimately save your life and the lives of others. Awareness is free. It never runs out and is issued to each and every person who walks the earth. Harnessing the power of awareness can be difficult and tiring, but with practice Total Awareness can become as natural as walking.

THE TOTAL AWARENESS™ SYSTEM

The Total Awareness (TA) System is a risk-assessment tool that manages and reduces threat vulnerabilities. The structured Total Awareness approach can be used by anyone at any time, but is designed specifically for the professional traveler—the diplomat, government employee, journalist, or businessperson.

Components of the Total Awareness System

The Total Awareness System can be broken down into a set of components that, taken together, create a complete awareness profile. These components include:

- **Situational Awareness (SA)**, *a conscious and constant focus on the environment* that seeks to detect, validate, and confirm threats. Your ability to detect potential threats should be a result of both instinct and observation. Chapter 2 will discuss situational awareness in detail.

- **Personal Awareness (PA)**, *the image and demeanor you project.* Your demeanor can increase your vulnerability to risk if you appear lost, confused, or simply out of your element. But honing your Personal Awareness can help you blend into a specific culture, reduce your threat exposure, and reduce your visibility to others—or it can increase your vulnerability to risk. Personal Awareness gives you the ability to assess and manage specific character traits that could potentially make you vulnerable. We'll discuss it in Chapter 3.

- **Cultural Awareness (CA)**, *the assessment and understanding of the culture in a specific geographic location*. This awareness component covers areas such as cultural-specific social protocol, etiquette, mannerisms, and gestures. By combining Cultural and Personal Awareness, you will gain the ability to blend into the local culture and avoid standing out as a potential target. Chapter 4 will cover Cultural Awareness.

- **Third-Party Awareness (3PA)**, *the general public's perception of you and your actions*. In a nutshell, when you feel like everyone is staring at you, they probably are. Third-Party Awareness extends to groups like citizens, law enforcement, criminals, and even terrorists residing in the host country. Reducing Third-Party Awareness requires you to blend into the environment using Personal Awareness (managing the way your image and demeanor are projected within a cultural setting) and Situational Awareness skillsets. We'll talk about 3PA in Chapter 5.

- **THREAT**® *is a risk-assessment tool* and an acronym that stands for Technological, Health, Raid, Environmental, Agency, and Terror threats in a specific geographic location. An educated global traveler will research and assess these threats before any international trip, so that they know in advance how to prepare their senses, adjust their Situational and Personal Awareness, and decrease their vulnerabilities. Chapter 6 will discuss THREATs in detail.

Even when you are effectively practicing the Total Awareness System—fully locked in, absorbing and processing the information all around you like Jason Bourne of *The Bourne Identity*—you can still be caught off guard by forces beyond your control. But what the Total Awareness System will allow you to do is speed up your reaction time and decision-making, so that even when you're surprised, you'll be primed for effective action. Understanding the components of awareness can help you take control of forces normally *out* of your control.

To implement the Total Awareness System, you will need to properly assess and research a specific destination, prepare your senses, and adapt your Personal Awareness traits. Once you are in an environment, you must begin to identify third parties and potential threats in an orderly fashion in a limited amount of time. To do this, you will follow a mental checklist (covered in detail in the following pages) that will enable you to manage the information you take in and make decisions based on instinct and observation.

Taking these steps will ultimately enable you to escape the wolf.

**Situational Awareness
(SA)**

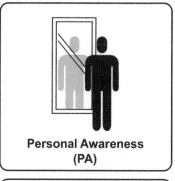

**Personal Awareness
(PA)**

**Cultural Awareness
(CA)**

**3rd Party Awareness
(3PA)**

SITUATIONAL AWARENESS

SITUATIONAL AWARENESS (SA)

SITUATIONAL AWARENESS ENABLES YOU TO FOCUS ON WHAT IS HAPPENING all around you. You take in all the information in your environment, recognizing how your own actions and the actions of others may influence the outcome.

Think about the difference between the experience of learning to drive a car and the way you have internalized the process now. You no longer hit the brake every time you see another car. You've learned to distinguish between false alarms and real threats, like the teenager who barrels through a red light or the car that is weaving all over the road ahead of you. Eventually, the process for detecting travel security and safety threats will become the same. Situational Awareness will help you keep your instinctively charged alerts in check with observed actions within the environment.

TYPES OF ENVIRONMENTS

As we start to learn about Situational Awareness, we must first define and understand the environment. The amount of control the local government has over crime, corruption, and other potential threats to the community and everyone in it—including you—is an important consideration in your planning. Your preparations for your trip to a country where the local government isn't strong, say a country like Mexico, will differ from the planning you would undertake when visiting a country where the local government is fairly strong, like the United Kingdom.

The US Government uses the following terminology to assess international travel threats:

- **Permissive environment**. An area that is completely controlled by the government. Its citizens support the government, and most importantly, the host government and its citizens support the United States. Utopia, if you will, where everyone lives in harmony. Not sure a fully permissive environment truly exists—Canada maybe?

- **Semi-permissive environment**. A government with questionable control. The citizens may or may not support the government. The government and citizens may or may not support the United States. Corruption is usually the wolf in these locations.

Country example: Indonesia. Most of the world is semi-permissive.

- **Nonpermissive environment.** An area where little or no government exists; sometimes called a denied area. Control is induced through the hostile actions of nongovernment forces. Support of the United States or its citizens is minimal. Country example: Afghanistan.

Note that though I defined each environment as an area, and used countries as examples, all three environments can exist within one country, province, or city, and an environment can change from permissive to semi-permissive or even nonpermissive at any moment.

You will want to research the area that you will be traveling to. What sort of environment(s) are you likely to encounter? Law enforcement research is paramount, because some of the most prolific criminals in semi-permissive countries are the police. Police corruption is a specific form of police misconduct in which the crimes are usually financially orientated and harmless. The most common form of corruption is the solicitation of or acceptance of bribes. If you travel to our closest threat country, Mexico, chances are high that you will be stopped by the police and "fined" exactly what happens to be in your wallet. In some countries, the police play large roles in the trafficking of drugs, humans, and terrorists. So beware and research your destination.

OODA LOOP

When you are stressed and time crunched, it's hard to make good decisions about what you've observed in your Situational Awareness—so I've incorporated a tactical decision-making process called the OODA loop (**O**bservation, **O**rientation, **D**ecision, and **A**ction).

Found in dozens of military and business strategy books, the OODA loop was developed by John Boyd, a US Air Force fighter pilot. Boyd had a standing bet with his fellow pilots; he bet that he could lock on a missile within forty seconds, even from a disadvantage, and if he lost, he'd pay forty dollars, a fair chunk of change during his time. According to legend, "Forty Second" Boyd never lost, in large part because of his decision-making process.

Boyd hypothesized that all intelligent organisms and organizations undergo a continuous cycle of interaction with their environment. He described four interrelated and overlapping processes through which an organism continuously cycles in a loop he believed to be critical to survival. The components of the OODA loop are:

- **Observation.** The collection of information or data by means of the senses.

- **Orientation.** The analysis and computation of the collected information and data observed to form a real-time mental perspective.

- **Decision**. The course of action to be taken based on your current orientation.

- **Action**. The physical play-out of the decision.

Practical Travel Example

Say you are away on business in a semi-permissive environment in the city of New Delhi in India. Your hotel is only a few blocks away from the location of the company you are going to meet with. Since you are running late, you decide to walk and skip the traffic jams. There is a shortcut, the same alley that your dinner companion from the night before used. It will save you precious time. But the alley is not well lit, and you think you see some movement. Should you go in, or take the longer way across an open square? You only have a few moments to make a quick decision. You know that in most instances, you can handle yourself. But is this a case where you want to gamble?

Using the OODA loop, you would *observe* by surveying the alley and the shadowy movement. Then you would *orient* by analyzing the data, both the research you've done before your trip and the visual survey you've just completed. Using the same common sense you would at home, you then *decide*, choosing the safer, more open route. And, you would complete the loop by *acting*, actually walking across the square and avoiding the alley and the potential robber.

After all, would you venture into an alley alone in New York City? We should always be especially cautious in known target areas for crime, like train stations, poorly lit areas, alleys, market sites, and crowded areas.

Boyd's loop is a commonsense approach. It's also an elegant framework for creating a competitive advantage. Not only can you observe, orient, decide, and act, but you can also get inside the head of your opponent's OODA loop. It's what basketball players do when they fake a move on the court. Imagine operating "inside" the wolf's OODA loop, so you can outthink and outmaneuver threats. In this case, the wolf in the alley has observed you. He noted the way you oriented yourself, scanning the alley, making a smart decision, and acting on it. He knows that you are a sheepdog and leaves you alone.

OODA Loop

OBSERVATION

Potential Threat observed ahead.

ORIENTATION

Two routes have been identified. Option A being the most direct route, but also most dangerous, or Option B, which is the longer but safer route.

ACTION

The longer but safer route is taken.

DECISION

Option B is ultimately the best course of action for safety.

Each stage of the loop relates to the other, leading to a speedy tactical decision. The OODA loop prevents action without planning—and as everyone knows, the difference between handling an emergency and descending into chaos is having a plan.

If you decide to read some of Boyd's theories, be warned that he did a great job of making something as simple and straight-forward as the OODA loop the equivalent to rocket science.

You remember Orange Alert? We see it all the time, for terrorist, environmental, or whatever other threats may come up. Orange is one of Cooper's Colors—a color-coded system of awareness. But let me ask you this—do you know where on that color spectrum orange lies? Is it really bad? Or just kind of bad?

We can't remember what all these colors are supposed to mean, because they're overly complicated. I like simple. In my opinion, simple is good, particularly when it comes to survival. The less there is to remember, the better.

THE MODES OF AWARENESS CYCLE

And this is simple. How do you screen out false alarms from real threats? The best way is through an approach that I call the **Modes of Awareness (MOA)** cycle. It is a continuum of alertness, which can be divided into three stages—*Alert, Pre-Crisis,* and *Crisis.* You can shift from mode to mode by the second, minute, hour, or day, depending on the perceived threat and the environment around you.

In a wolf-rich environment, your senses of feeling, sight, smell, and sound are your best assets. The pressure of a hand against your wallet, the smell of smoke, the sight of a crowd, or the sound of a gunshot should all cause you to move into the next appropriate phase of the Modes of Awareness cycle.

Here are the Modes of Awareness—Alert, Pre-Crisis, and Crisis—defined:

Alert Mode
Potential Time in Mode: *Hours, Days, Months*

Alert Mode involves constant observation of your environment, perpetually scanning for potential threats. You should be in Alert Mode the majority of the time you are traveling—in fact, ideally, a crisis will not arise and you should never have to switch out of Alert Mode. But transitioning from Alert to Pre-Crisis Mode will get triggered by the recognition of potential threats. Use the OODA loop to help you decide on the appropriate invisible threshold for making that transition:

You are in Alert Mode. You are identifying, positioning, and acting based on POTENTIAL threats.

- **Observation**. You are feeling, looking, listening, and smelling your environment.

- **Orientation**. You are mentally changing your position based on the information being collected and processed from potential threats.

- **Decision**. You are constantly making decisions to mitigate any potential threats.

- **Action**. You are acting on the decisions to maintain the greatest advantage over perceived potential threats. You are deliberately trying to confirm potential threats.

So what does this look like in daily life? Say I'm at the grocery store. I'm not just checking the grocery list on my phone, and I'm not just checking prices on the shelves—I'm also paying attention to the person in front of me, the person behind me, and everybody who is crossing each aisle.

Or say I'm at the gas station. Yeah, I'm filling up my car, but I'm not just clicking the button and leaving the nozzle to do the work while I scroll through my phone. I'm paying attention to the person on the other side of the pump and to the cars driving around looking for a place to pull in.

Alert Mode is reminding yourself to pay attention to everything around you, even when things are totally normal, and even when you're in the middle of a task. If I'm at a drive-through, I'm watching the cars in front of me and behind me until I've got my coffee and I'm well on my way.

Pre-Crisis Mode

Potential Time in Mode: *Minutes, Hours*

Pre-Crisis Mode is the constant observation of identified potential threats. It allows a person to determine courses of action, and designates an invisible threshold that activates Crisis Mode. The decisions made in this mode allow you to be in the best position should Crisis Mode become necessary.

In Pre-Crisis, you are identifying, positioning, and acting based on CONFIRMED threat(s).

- **Observation.** You feel, see, hear, or smell the confirmed threat(s).

- **Orientation.** You are physically and mentally changing your position to gain the greatest advantage over the confirmed threat(s).

- **Decision.** You are constantly reevaluating the environment, developing courses of action to increase your odds of mitigation and escape from the confirmed threat(s).

- **Action.** You are setting invisible thresholds that will initiate Crisis Mode if breached by the threat(s). You are evaluating the situation to prepare for Crisis Mode.

Pre-Crisis Mode occurs when there's a trigger in the

environment indicating that something may or may not happen. Going back to the grocery store, that might mean I hear a couple yelling and screaming at each other in the next aisle. I've got to ask myself, is this going to get violent? The situation is not necessarily going to affect me, but it's enough of a trigger for me to pause my task and consider the situation. Where are my outs? Will I need an improvised weapon?

Or if I'm at the gas pump and I hear a collision—where is it? What got hit?

Crisis Mode
Potential Time in Mode: *Seconds, Minutes*

Crisis Mode is when you take tactical action against the threat. At this stage, your goal is to elude, escape, or dominate the threat so you can quickly and successfully transition back to Pre-Crisis Mode. It's no time for decision-making, which should have been completed in Pre-Crisis Mode. Crisis Mode is triggered by the breach of the invisible threshold you have set in Pre-Crisis mode, and your goal is to transition back to Pre-Crisis Mode sooner rather than later. Prolonged exposure to the threat may decrease survivability.

You are actively ENGAGED with the threat(s). In full-on crisis mode, you are attacking, defending yourself against, or escaping the threat(s). You are identifying, positioning, and acting against the threat(s) to return to Pre-Crisis Mode as quickly as possible.

- **Observation**. You are feeling, looking, listening, and smelling for a Pre-Crisis environment.

- **Orientation**. You are physically and mentally changing your position based on the information being processed in the Crisis Mode.

- **Decision**. You are constantly making decisions that will mitigate or eliminate the threat(s).

- **Action**. You are acting out the decisions that will enable you to defeat the threat, survive, and return to Pre-Crisis Mode.

In the grocery store, my best action is to leave through one of the exits I identified in Pre-Crisis. I'm not going to get into a physical altercation with anybody—but I am calling 911.

At the gas station, I am moving away from my vehicle. I don't want to be anywhere near something that might explode while I ensure that it's not a gas pump that just got run over.

-Senses Focused
-No Time Limit

Alert

-Peak Stress
-Seconds / Minutes

Crisis

-Added Stress
-Minutes / Hours

Pre-Crisis

MODES OF AWARENESS

Practical Travel Example

Let's use another real-life travel example to illustrate how the MOA cycle works. Africa. I'm up early, before the sun. The day starts out like every other in my three-month assignment in the city. To get a head start on work, I plan to get in early. I turn the key to the rental SUV and the engine springs to life, breaking

the deathly stillness. The only other sound is the low hum of a
rudimentary power line in my temporary housing. I pull out of
the driveway, breathe in the cool, dry air, and survey the narrow
dirt road ahead. My headlights illuminate the sultry blackness.
Even though it's early and I haven't had my coffee yet, I'm in
Awareness Mode, paying attention to everything I see.

The first three miles of my trip into the city never vary. No
choice—there aren't any turn-offs or side streets, just this
single, bumpy lane. Even without traffic, it's slow going,
splashing through rain-filled potholes. Less than a mile into
this familiar trek, I notice a man with his back to me, sitting on
a motorcycle with no lights on, parked in a residential driveway along the lane. It's a little odd, but nothing out of the ordinary. During my time here, I've noticed that Africans tend to
be up at all times of night. Second mile into my trip, a car with
its hood up is smack in the middle of the roadway. A second
car sits behind it. I'm about 500 yards away, going downhill.
At that moment, a single headlight bounces off my rearview
mirror. It's the motorcycle. The second car pulls next to the
car with the raised hood. Now the entire road is blocked.
Immediately I switch into Pre-Crisis Mode and begin evaluating possible decisions. Should I stop here? There is someone
behind me and in front of me. Others could be lurking in the
tree line to my right and left. Do I throw my car into reverse
and head back the way I came, recognizing that my escape
options are limited? Or should I keep the momentum going
and go for broke?

My assailants are counting on me to behave like most people. So I decide to change the game. In a hostile environment, it's best to react with extreme caution. You never know how many threats there really are or if some ambush is already in full place.

Shifting immediately into Crisis Mode, I choose to hit the gas and drive toward the two cars, which now have their high-beam headlights trained on me. At the last moment, I cut left and drive up a forty-five-degree embankment, missing the other vehicle by inches and knocking off my mirror in the process. I take the option they didn't expect—coming right at them. As a result, I catch them off guard, and go on my merry way.

* * *

A multilevel, personal-crisis management system can increase awareness, confirm threats, and prevent victimization, compromise, and even death. The transfers from mode to mode (Alert, Pre-Crisis, and Crisis) depend heavily on two identified stages of the OODA loop, *observation* and *decision*. Both are instrumental in guiding the most effective action against a variety of threats.

THE POWER OF OBSERVATION

As you'll have noted, the Modes of Awareness cycle is steered by observation. Observation is a skill, one that will make you a safer, more secure traveler. It helps you assess the environment, identify potential risks or threats, and either find ways to avoid those threats or plan avenues of escape. Highly dependent on the body's senses (sight, hearing, and to a lesser degree, smell), observation plays a critical role in a crisis.

Observation is not the same as looking. It's active, and it requires conscious effort on your part. By focusing your mind on a particular element in your environment, whether it's a fact, event, or person, observation allows you to recognize and retain that fact and recall it in the future. It's the perception of shapes, size, and features. Colors, shades, and lighting. Speed, time, and distance. It consists of three processes: *attention, perception*, and *retention*.

Attention

Attention is most critical during Alert or Pre-Crisis mode. Without attention, perception and retention are impossible. For most people, attention is limited to items and events with a direct bearing on the current activity. If you are driving down the road, your attention is mostly focused on what's in front of you, though your involuntary attention may be captured by something out of the ordinary, like a truck with garbage falling out the back. Or, if you're walking through a crowd, a person with a limp may draw your attention. Very large or small people, bright colors, and sharp or loud sounds have the same effect. But the reality is that sometimes the things you most need to pay attention to are actively trying *not* to stand out. The Modes of Awareness cycle and the OODA loop will help broaden the range of your attention. This greater span of attention is important in building your Situational Awareness so you can identify potential threats.

Perception

Perception is heavily influenced by your experience, background, and education. People tend to perceive and remember only the familiar or what interests them. Here again, your ability to expand observation beyond ingrained habits requires a conscious effort. Your mind will tend to filter out items subconsciously when you don't have a frame of reference to help retain them for subsequent retrieval. To improve your powers of observation, you'll want to be aware of these tendencies.

Retention

Retention must be practiced. People have a tendency to remember what they want and forget everything else. We need to train our brains, just like our bodies, to be adept at particular skills. Retention skills and recall go hand in hand. Being able to remember details will help you when it comes time to report a crime. Even if the crime in question didn't happen to you, you'll be able to give details that might save someone's life.

Retention can also help you detect whether or not you're under surveillance (more on that in Chapter 5). You won't be able to tell if someone's following you unless you can remember what everyone around you looks like in the first place. Is that the exact same car, or is it just a similar make and model? Is it the same person driving, or someone different? These details will help you differentiate between true surveillance and an overactive imagination.

Beyond that, a good memory allows you to be more heads-up in your life. If you don't have to check your phone constantly to remember your next appointment or check how to get somewhere, you can keep your eyes in front of you, paying attention.

A couple of techniques can enhance your ability to retain details. You can use the mind-image association techniques that are practiced in Dale Carnegie seminars, along with other memory aids. These techniques stack strong imagery and mental associations with repetition, as follows:

- Create a strong mental *picture or association* with the item. It helps if the mental association is something that resonates with you, even if it's nonsensical to someone else. For example, if the person you want to remember looks like your twelfth-grade English teacher, then consciously make that association. You'll remember that she had blonde hair and was slim, just like Mrs. Dye.

33

- To improve your recall in general, practice *serial association*:

  * Create a vivid mental picture for a list of items, say fifteen or so, which you will have to recall in order. You can do this by assigning meaning to each item.

  * For example, say you have to remember articles of clothing. Start with a tie, and imagine it is red and choking someone, causing them to turn red in the face. Next up is a pair of green high heels, which you associate with a Day-Glo green color. The heels are slipping up and down, causing blisters on the person's feet. The third item might be a hat. Think of a French beret with a striking black-and-white houndstooth pattern, which is moving all around so that it causes you to feel dizzy.

  * If you use this type of vivid imagery, associated with all five of your senses, it will be much easier to recall a long list of items, or the faces or names of individuals. So if you need to remember the person who reminds you of Mrs. Dye, use your imagination to add those emotional components that engage all of your senses.

- *Repeat* the mental picture over and over, or say someone's name over and over.

Keep In Mind (KIM) drills are great for increasing observation and retention performance. This training drill is used in sniper-related military training and requires a partner to set up several different objects, in a particular order, spread out within a designated environment. You then have a limited amount of time to observe and retain the details of the pre-staged environment. Once the time is up, you must write down everything observed and sketch exactly where each item was located. Doing this regularly increases your ability to observe and retain small details.

KIM (Keep in Mind) Drill

| Observe for 30 seconds and then cover with your hand. | How many details can you remember? |

As mentioned previously, you need to pay attention to perceive and retain information. Remember, too, that perception can play games with you. Most people use Hollywood and the media as their frame of reference for what a threat looks like, but in reality this type of reference limits you. Often, real threats are unassuming and invisible in the environment—they're not trying to stand out like a movie star. Don't filter out the real threats because of false stereotypes. Be as concerned about the baby-faced teenager who is hanging out (and probably eyeing your purse or wallet) as you are the hulking "foreigner."

AREAS OF OBSERVATION

Let's take a closer look at observation by breaking down all the identifiable information for a specific threat. Say the threat is surveillance, which is increasingly a real issue for business travelers. A businessperson may be watched by those who are interested in proprietary company information or an unsavory character plotting a kidnapping for ransom.

With surveillance detection, the primary objective is to identify or confirm that you are under surveillance. But that can be a lot more complicated and difficult than you might think. Years ago, I was in a third-world country validating that a team was still conducting active surveillance of a particular country's embassy. Basically, locals had been hired to "hang out" in the embassy vicinity and report any unusual behavior, and I was trying to figure out if they were actually doing their job. But this proved difficult because, from a distance, each member looked exactly the same. They were all clean-shaven Africans with well-groomed hair who wore slacks and collared shirts, drove taxis, and mingled among other people with similar features and clothing. I couldn't stare at them or get up close, or I would have been identified as a possible threat and reported. That would have been bad.

So, I had to find specific characteristics to identify each individual person. One guy wore the same shirt almost every day. Another always squatted in the same spot. Others I associated with the taxi they drove. This took weeks of paying attention and observing their patterns.

Observed Characteristics

Identifying a multimember surveillance team takes a considerable amount of observation, and involves the ability to retain the characteristics of these members even as they travel in a sea of other people. If you're being followed, or suspect you're being followed, you will want to try to remember key characteristics about that person. This will help you confirm if you are encountering that same individual again and again, or if it's just people with similar characteristics. I'm not suggesting you remember everyone around you—that's just not feasible. Instead, note the individual that you suspect, and focus in on their dominant characteristics, the ones that are difficult to alter. Don't waste time memorizing useless information, like the color of their shirt. Unlike that one guy I was watching, most people change their shirt all the time. Develop an overall mental image of the individual, and key in on the retainable features, the ones they can't change. Once you start learning to categorize these features during observation, they become easier to retain and identify in the future.

The dominant characteristics to retain are *feature* and *form*. Body features consist primarily of face, head, and hair. Three things that directly impact these are gender, race, and age, although these are not considered features in and of themselves because none of them can stand alone as an identifiable characteristic for surveillance detection. Body features are the most accurate characteristics to help you identify individuals. With exception of hair color, these are generally the most difficult and time consuming to alter. Body features, however, are the most difficult to observe because they require you to be close enough to scrutinize the individual.

Take note of the following:

Observation of form includes the shape, build, and size of an individual. Any prominent physical aspect can be isolated for retention purposes. The overall body shape is made up of the trunk, arms, and legs. Keep in mind that how clothing fits can distort your perception of body shape. Size is relative to overall body shape but can be distorted by distance. Doors and doorways make great reference points when determining approximate height. Once again, distance can distort perception of height. Finally, posture can have a significant effect on overall form. This is a mannerism or demeanor trait.

Tight Clothes:
Appears tall and thin

Baggy Clothes:
Appears big and bulky

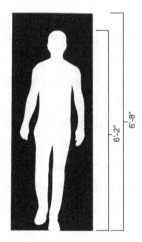

Actual size :
In relation to door frame

Observation of Form

Demeanor, particularly mannerisms, are characteristics or idiosyncrasies that are unique to an individual and easily retained. Peculiarities in action or bearing, or in posture, stride, pace of motion, or voice quality. Individual demeanor is established through myriad mannerisms, and they are either programmed over a lifetime or result from physical characteristics. Those developed over a lifetime become subconscious actions and therefore can only be controlled by conscious effort.

Mannerisms that result from physical characteristics are much more difficult to alter because the mind cannot control or conceal what the body is unable to. For this reason, mannerisms are one of the most important key traits to observe during surveillance. Most other traits can be concealed or disguised, but mannerisms take serious, conscious effort. Stride and posture are the easiest to observe and recognize again at a later location. Another is someone's personality trait. For example, extroverts display a more outgoing, positive, or aggressive demeanor. These characteristics are difficult to disguise or conceal in the heat of surveillance. Yes, sometimes wolves can affect mannerisms that are not their own, but this isn't the movies. We aren't talking about Keyser Söze from *The Usual Suspects* here, and while faking a limp isn't that hard, remembering to be consistent with your stride or body language is beyond most people.

Items people use and keep for a longer period of time, or **longevity items**, can also be observable points. These include things like backpacks, bags, shoes, purses, belts, or other props a surveillance operator would wear or carry. Surveillance personnel may change clothes, disguises, or wigs, but they very rarely will take time to change shoes, belts, purses, or bags. Typically, surveillance personnel carry cameras and other technical devices. Switching gear from one bag to another is time consuming. Watches are also worth paying attention to, because surveillance operators wear watches and typically don't think to switch those out.

Surveillance is only one threat of many where observation is key. If you thoroughly identify traits unique to a potential threat and retain the images for later use, you can piece together much of the overall threat picture.

Observation is a grossly overlooked, yet vital, element to survival. Observation steers transitions between Alert, Pre-Crisis, and Crisis modes, assesses the environment, identifies threats, and finds avenues of escape.

DECISION-MAKING

Let's now turn to the next element that drives the transition from one mode of awareness to another: **decisions.** I am not talking about ordinary, run-of-the-mill decisions, which are usually made with the luxury of time and in a relaxed environment. Rather, this is a specific subset of tactical decision-making, which is called **Naturalistic Decision-Making (NDM).**

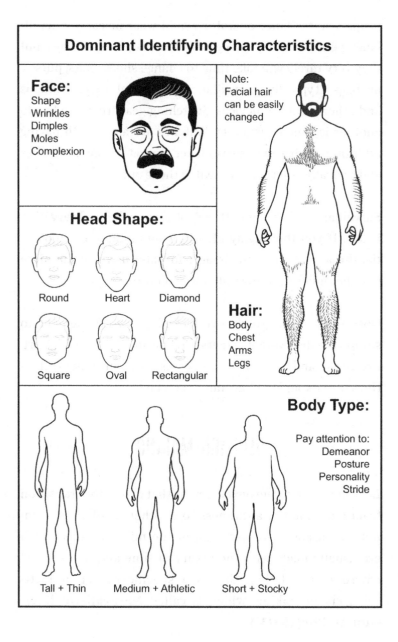

By definition, Naturalistic Decision-Making is used when stakes are high, time is crunched, and stress is abundant. Decisions drive actions, and those actions determine your ability to be a safe and secure world traveler.

Dr. Michael Uttaro, a retired FBI agent and chief executive officer of Tactical Operations Support Services, is an expert on this type of decision-making. His research lays out the scientific aspects of Naturalistic Decision-Making, and you will note how NDM supports Situational Awareness as defined under the Total Awareness System.

Naturalistic Decision-Making

Uttaro states that every day, we:

> ...make a number of decisions which, when placed on a continuum, range from very easy to extremely difficult. Many of these decisions can be considered routine and are made in a manner that does not require a considerable amount of thought or effort. Other decisions, however, require intensive deliberation; their consequences have a profound influence over many lives. Take, for example, the decision-making associated with the aftermath of September 11, and the lives affected by the decisions that readied this nation for war. It is these types of judgments and decisions that most interest researchers.

This new paradigm, labeled "naturalistic decision-making," provides a description of decision-making as it unfolds in a field setting and "rejects a purely formal approach, whether for describing or for evaluating decisions."

The field of naturalistic decision-making focuses on situational awareness, planning, and other cognitive functions that emerge in natural settings instead of in a controlled laboratory setting. Consider the experience of Captain Chesley "Sully" Sullenberger, who landed his damaged plane in the Hudson River. His decision saved the lives of his passengers and crew—but it was still called into question by his superiors, because in a controlled setting, no one made the exact same decision. Captain Sullenberger pointed out that this was *not* a controlled situation. Naturalistic decision-making exists outside of controlled situations, in the real world with real stakes. It is critical in occupations such as air traffic control, the military, firefighting, surgery, and others where high-risk decisions need to be made quickly.

As Uttaro goes on to say:

> Under true conditions, you often avoid situations that are ambiguous and in a state of chaos and disorder. **To better make a decision, the recognition of detail is accomplished mainly by observation**, which gets contextual meaning through the analytical and intuitive processes.

Another decision-making tool, "intuitive messenger," is the ubiquitous hunches or "gut feelings" that are so often associated with effective policing. **Research has shown that intuition, as a whole, strongly influences one's decision-making/judgment competency and proficiency**...One problem lies in our inability to properly listen to these omnipresent intuitive signals when rendering decisions. The consequence of ignoring the "intuitive messengers" during criminal encounters could prove costly for victims and officers because **calm, thoughtful, and rational decision-making can hardly function under situations of violence and uncertainty**.

Essentially, in the real world, we don't have time to think through the various possibilities and repercussions of all the possible decisions we might make. All we can do is observe, trust our intuition, and move forward.

Decision-Making Preparation

That said, we definitely want to increase our chances of making *good* decisions in the moment. One factor that contributes greatly toward the effectiveness of the decision-making process is extensive preparation, and my Total Awareness System is all about being prepared.

As Uttaro says:

> Preparation is considered a fundamental task, essential in producing positive results, but is often overlooked or at least neglected. Preparation is the filling in of the details, the development of possible routes, the recognition of potential barriers, and the construction of options.

Without preparation, you are left to draw only on *experience*, and you react in an information vacuum. This limits your options to choices that you have already made in the past. Experience, or more appropriately, a lack of experience, limits the skillset needed to anticipate and react to a "surprise."

Experience can greatly assist in the development of "what if's" and in the construction of worst-case scenarios. These worst-case scenarios are the trigger points or barriers that cause you to change course or shift modes during a dynamic event. But in the heat of the moment, they can never adequately substitute for the preparation of a range of potential responses.

Preparation involves several stages, including activities undertaken prior to your trip and activities that can be done while traveling. Before traveling, you need to gather as much knowledge and awareness about the location or impending situation as possible. The smallest detail could prove very beneficial when barriers are encountered and alternatives need to be explored. Consider as many worst-case scenarios as possible and think through the consequences associated with each scenario. This also serves as a preventive mechanism to avoid potentially bad decisions when action is eventually required.

This level of detail provides the input that you will need to construct an internal cognitive map. Unanticipated or unpredicted scenarios do occur in real life. How ready will you be to respond to these events? That will depend on how thoroughly you have prepared, and how often you have reviewed and evaluated the ongoing and unfolding "situation."

Decision-making is about more than what shoes are to be worn for the day, especially when the wolf comes prowling.

> "I come in here and the first thing I'm doing is catching the sidelines and looking for an exit...I can tell you the license plate on all six cars outside; our waitress is left-handed and the guy sitting up at the counter is 215 pounds and knows how to handle himself. I know the best place to look for a gun is in the cab of the gray truck outside. And at this altitude I can run flat-out for a half mile before my hands start to shake. Why would I know that?"
>
> —JASON BOURNE, *Bourne Identity*, 2002.

If only it were that simple!

> "The first condition of understanding a foreign country is to smell it."
>
> —RUDYARD KIPLING

CHAPTER 2 REVIEW

PRACTICE ASSIGNMENT

MODES OF AWARENESS CYCLE

IN THIS SECTION, WE'VE TACKLED THE IMPORTANT CONCEPTS OF Situational Awareness and the supporting Modes of Awareness. Situational Awareness *is a conscious and constant focus on the environment* that seeks to detect, validate, and confirm threats. Your ability to detect potential threats can result from natural instinct, but can also be developed as a skill. Situational Awareness is a habit of mind. Like any other intentional habit, it takes time to develop and should be approached as a way of life.

As a way of practicing that skill, let's see how you would apply the Modes of Awareness and OODA concepts to the scenario below.

PRACTICAL EXAMPLE

- Semi-permissive environment (area with limited government control)

- Visiting on assignment with a colleague who knows the local environment

In this scenario, you are traveling on assignment in Mexico. You've made arrangements with the local lead and feel comfortable with the information he has supplied. He picks you up at the Mexico City airport. Using Situational Awareness, you've done your homework and recognize that it will be important to be cautious because both Americans and Mexicans are vulnerable to crime and the risk of kidnapping in Mexico City.

During the ride from the airport, you discuss the overall security situation with your colleague, gaining additional information. Your associate drops you off at your hotel, in a nice part of town. You are in **Alert Mode,** in the *observation* stage of the OODA loop process, scanning the environment for potential threats. You are orienting yourself to the environment, both on the ride and as you survey your hotel room. You make a note of the individuals in the hotel, the check-in and check-out procedures, the fire emergency process, and any potential threats.

After a successful meeting, you return to your hotel. In the lobby, a uniformed man approaches you. He stops you and indicates that he is with the local police force and needs to speak with you.

STUDY GUIDE QUESTIONS

What should you do next? Are you still in Alert Mode? Why or why not?

Do you think this person is a threat? Why or why not? How would you determine this?

What do you think happens in this scenario?

STUDY GUIDE ANSWERS

What should you do next? Are you still in Alert Mode? Why or why not?

Did you continue with your OODA loop process? You should absolutely still be in Alert Mode, and so the next step would be to make a *decision,* as there won't be much time for decision-making in the *Pre-Crisis* and *Crisis Modes.* You should also be setting the *invisible thresholds* that will determine a shift into Pre-Crisis mode.

You decide that your invisible threshold will be breached if the individual tries to forcibly take you somewhere. You are also making decisions at this point about what you will do if this person *does* try to take you somewhere. You are getting ready to *act*, to shift to Pre-Crisis, if the invisible threshold is crossed.

Do you think this person is a threat? Why or why not? How would you determine this?

Good research can help give you a head start about potential threats like this one. Instinct also comes into play. Assuming you did your preparation before traveling, you will have learned of recent incidents in which impersonators donned uniforms to perpetrate a crime. Your instincts are telling you that something just doesn't seem right.

All that information is being pulled together in the *orient* step of the OODA loop. In this case, the uniformed individual grabs your arm and tries to move you toward the door of the hotel. He is saying something unintelligible about going to the police station. Yep, a *confirmed* threat. Your invisible threshold has been breached, and you shift into *Pre-Crisis Mode*.

What do you think happens in this scenario?

The uniformed individual begins to make a scene. Americans hate scenes, and most will comply with orders in order to put a halt to a heated interaction. But if you have quickly run through the Observe, Orient, Decide, and Act process and determined the individual's behavior to be a trap, his behavior will trigger you to shift from *Pre-Crisis* to *Crisis Mode*. You will *act* based on the decisions you made in Pre-Alert Mode—which is to do something unexpected.

You pull your arm away and walk quickly toward the hotel's front desk. You pull out your cell phone and call your colleague. The uniformed individual comes after you. You remain calm but keep walking to stay ahead of him. You explain the situation to your colleague to make sure someone else knows what is happening.

You reach the hotel's front desk, making sure a number of people are around as witnesses. You request assistance and explain you do not think this person is really a police officer. Suddenly, the uniformed individual disappears. The threat is over—for now. Your homework and your ability to analyze and respond quickly to a potential threat have served you well. What was it all about? Most likely, it was a potential kidnapping scheme. Thanks to thorough preparation, and the ability to process information quickly using the Modes of Awareness cycle and the OODA loop, you were able to elude this threat. Congratulations!

HOW POWERS OF OBSERVATION CAN SAVE YOUR WALLET AND A LOT MORE

In this chapter, we also explored how observation and Naturalistic Decision-Making can help enhance your awareness of the environment around you. Now, let's see how to apply those skills to a hypothetical situation.

PRACTICAL EXAMPLE

- Semi-permissive environment
  (area with some government control)

- Family vacation

When I was a kid, my dad worked in Saudi Arabia for ARAMCO, one of the most powerful oil companies in the world. Every year the company provided employees with $5,000 per family member to go on vacation for thirty days, which was not a bad deal. The real reason for the stipend was to give us a chance to renew our visas. (The Saudis would only allow foreigners eleven-month visas. Don't ask me why—no clue.)

One summer, we ended up in Rome, and it was incredibly hot. My dad enjoyed walking everywhere, although the rest of the family (me, my mom, and little brother) would have preferred a taxi. That particular day, we were walking toward St. Peter's Basilica to see the Pope perform his daily ritual of water sprinkling, hand waving, and baby kissing.

We trudged on in the scorching heat as drops of sweat rolled off our skin. As we crossed a bridge, our little family passed a group of about ten children, ranging in age from about six to ten years. They were playing sidewalk games. As we approached, the children started crying and begging for money, food, and water. They began to tug on me, my mom, the stroller (with my brother in it), and my dad, all the while making signs for food, water, and money. The minute we passed through their gauntlet, the crowd went quiet.

Suddenly my dad yelled, "They took my wallet!"

He forced them to the wall of the bridge and continued to shout, "Wallet, wallet, give me my wallet!"

My mom then started to scream, "Polieeze, polieeze!"

My dad turned to me and bellowed, "Clint, start kicking their butts!"

I was nine. I did nothing of the sort. I just held onto the stroller with my brother inside and watched my parents freak out. Entertaining to say the least.

Eventually, the wallet came flying from the center of the crowd of kids and landed on the sidewalk. The cop on the corner just watched as well. The world loves Americans!

STUDY GUIDE QUESTIONS

How did my dad know his wallet had been taken? After all, the begging and tugging were great distractions.

Let's do a little quiz to see how well you recall some of the details of the scene I just described. How many children were there? What was their approximate age range? What time of year was it? How many people were in my family? Who were they? How old was I? What did the policeman do?

STUDY GUIDE ANSWERS

How did my dad know his wallet had been taken?

How did my dad know that his wallet had been taken? It was because he was literally sweating his butt off. The cool breeze that suddenly visited his back pocket cued him in immediately. He was using one of his five senses—his sense of feel. This power of observation helped our family out and saved his wallet and its contents.

After that, my dad came up with a great anti-pickpocket trick. Dad always carried a pocket comb to tidy up his hair, or what was left of it. He inserted the plastic comb lengthwise in the fold of his bifold wallet with the teeth up. That simple move made it impossible for the wallet to come out of his pocket without the comb teeth getting hung up on the pocket interior. It was great fun watching him pay for stuff. Every time he had to extract his wallet from his back pocket, he would tug away and curse the whole time, but his wallet was always there.

Recall quiz: How many children were there? What was their approximate age range? What time of year was it? How many people were in my family? Who were they? How old was I? What did the policeman do?

Let's check your observation and memory skills. There were ten kids, from about six to ten years in age. It was summer— did the details about the sweat help you remember that part? There were four people in my family: my dad, my mom, my little brother, and me. I was nine. As for the policeman, he just watched the show.

With practice, you'll be able to enhance powers of observation and decision-making. Those skills can come in very handy in helping you detect potential threats while you are traveling, but they can be just as important when you are in your hometown or negotiating at a business meeting.

NOTES:

PERSONAL AWARENESS

"Travel can be one of the most rewarding forms of introspection."

—LAWRENCE DURRELL

Personal Awareness (PA) is the image and demeanor you project to the public.

You have the ability to increase your own self-awareness, and as a result, manage how you are perceived by others. This power allows you to blend in within a specific culture, reducing threat vulnerabilities and keeping you off the radar of criminals, other bad guys, and the general public (Third-Party Awareness). Personal Awareness is the most important aspect of the Total Awareness System, and it should always be guided by the culture of your destination.

Using Personal Awareness, you will assess and manage specific character traits that might separate you from the culture you will be visiting, shifting your demeanor until you blend in. You will need to identify your personal vulnerabilities and exposures based on the host country environment. What do I mean by personal vulnerabilities and exposures? The following example provides a good illustration.

WHEN SHEEPDOGS MUST DRESS LIKE SHEEP

During World War II, a joint operation was launched in Nazi-occupied territories. British Special Operations Executive, the US Office of Strategic Services, and the French Bureau Central de Renseignements et d'Action together conducted sabotage and guerrilla warfare, and led the French Foreign Resistance. These operations were directed by three-man teams, usually composed of an American, a Frenchman, and a British operative. The three-man multinational unit would parachute into enemy territory to train, equip, organize, and lead pockets of civilians on raids against Nazi targets. These operations were code-named "Jedburgh."

Such missions required a very deliberate and thorough training pipeline. Most volunteers were seasoned World War II soldiers with combat experience, language skills, radio operator experience, and leadership skills. The training consisted of parachuting, land navigation, clandestine radio operations, weapons, explosives, tactics, and basic tradecraft (also known as spycraft). Although the training was exceptional for its time, it lacked a few valuable lifesaving skills that would have helped these operatives blend into the local environments.

In some areas of operation, Jedburgh team members had to pose as French citizens, living, working, and eating together with Nazis. The Jedburgh members had to dress, walk, smell, and eat like Frenchmen—which was completely foreign to the American and British operatives. Because of this deficiency, several Jedburgh team members were identified as "different," questioned, taken prisoner, or executed on the spot.

One interview revealed that the Americans were unfamiliar with European dining customs. Americans hold their fork with their right hand and usually leave the knife on the table until it is required. When cutting, Americans switch the fork from their right to their left hand, pick up the knife with the right, and cut their food. When not cutting, the knife is put down, and the fork is used to carry the food to the mouth. Europeans use both the knife and fork the entire meal and never switch positions. Simple, little mistakes like this cost lives.

Similarly, the British operatives couldn't break the habit of pouring milk in their cup before adding hot tea. Other Europeans pour the hot tea into a cup first and then add milk. The British operatives would also look right, rather than left, before crossing the street, while Americans and French do the opposite. Knowing and using these local customs would have saved lives.

The Jedburghs were victims of personal habit and cultural difference. The saying "It's the little things" truly applies to this example. Now, breaking lifelong habits is difficult, but instead of thinking of it as trying to quit, it can be easier to consider temporarily replacing one habit with another that fits into the local culture. Creating a new habit still takes some effort. It takes eight days of constant reminders for 90 percent retention, twenty-one days to start a pattern, and one hundred days for a new action to become automatic. So don't think that those two days of practice prior to departure are going to set you up for success.

You might be thinking, "If it's going to take me one hundred days, what's the point? I'm not going to have that kind of lead time to prepare for every trip I take." Sure, that's true—you won't have that kind of time to work on place-specific details. But learning the general lifestyle of Personal Awareness? That you do have time for, and you should start *now*. These are skills that will serve you in every aspect of your life, no matter where you go. So get in the habit, until it becomes automatic.

WHY DISGUISE IS IMPORTANT

You may not be a clandestine operative, but you *will* be scrutinized and judged everywhere you travel. Depending on where you're going, you may think, "Why bother? I don't look remotely like the majority of people at my destination. I am going to stand out anyway."

That may be an accurate statement. The observing party, however, doesn't necessarily know that you are American. Based on your appearance and actions, you could present yourself as being European, Canadian, Australian, or South African.

This is unfortunate, but it's reality: Americans are more frequently targeted than some other nationalities. Toning down your American signatures will help reduce your vulnerabilities.

You have to live and breathe Personal Awareness through daily action, whether you are in the comfort of your own home or traveling abroad. Proper planning, research, and the constant injection of awareness into your daily life are a must. If an action is part of your lifestyle, it will appear natural to third parties when you are traveling in different environments.

Remember John Boyd, who developed the OODA loop, from Chapter 2? He divides warfare into three distinct elements: *moral warfare, mental warfare,* and *physical warfare. Moral warfare* destroys the enemy's will to win and breaks down fibers of trust within a unit. *Mental warfare* distorts the enemy's perception of reality through disinformation, posturing, and projection. Finally, *physical warfare* is the destruction of the enemy, enemy resources, and other assets.

Your projection and demeanor, a crucial part of Personal Awareness, is a form of mental warfare. Now, you may be a peace-loving person. You are probably thinking, "I don't want to wage war on anyone, and I certainly don't want to pick a fight when I am traveling abroad." Great, but that's not actually the point of Personal Awareness. We are talking about using deception to distort the perception of a potential predator—this form of mental warfare is not about picking a fight. It's about preventing one from happening in the first place.

And as it happens, this form of warfare sometimes involves acting meeker than you really are. Sometimes it pays for a sheepdog to pose as a sheep. Are there instances where this could give you the advantage? You better believe it. Presenting yourself as a tough guy might ward off wolves in Los Angeles, but my guess is that it wouldn't work in Northern Pakistan.

At the end of the day, culture is what drives projection and demeanor. The way I project myself in America is completely different from how I want to be perceived overseas. Here at home, I tend to dress like a tough guy. Tight T-shirt, sunglasses, adventure pants—all of that says former special ops, and I'm fine with that. Here in the US, someone sees that and they decide they don't want to mess with that guy, plus there's a certain level of respect and support for a veteran.

But outside the US? That look stands out, and the last thing I want is to be noticed. So instead I'm wearing a shirt that probably isn't so fitted and is nondescript, with no logos or brand names. I've got jeans and penny loafers, and I've taken off my fancy dive watch and replaced it with something I got for twenty dollars.

Domestic Wear   **International Wear**

This is how I employ the sheep, sheepdog, and wolf differently than Grossman. There are times when you must look like a sheepdog to ward off wolves. But when traveling with an array of sheep, while possibly having wolves all around you, it might be more beneficial to look like just another sheep. Again, it's about blending in.

Though downgrading aggression may sound easier than ramping it up, I must identify the single most important issue sheepdogs or alpha types will face. EGO! Americans, as a whole, are very egotistical. Collapsing the ego and pretending to become a sheep is the most difficult task at hand for many of us. Vanity must be set aside. We all want to look pretty, or cool, or tough, but these presentations will make us targets. Unless, of course, you like that kind of attention. Then, by all means, start your day in an orange jumpsuit!

Remember, this book is dedicated to reducing your vulnerabilities and increasing your awareness across the board. It's about escaping the wolf, not beating him up. Whether you are a diplomat, government operative, or business traveler, blending in is better than standing out.

I tell students, all alpha males and gods in their own worlds, to put on penny loafers and a calculator watch, stop using hair products, and start wearing clothes from Goodwill. The looks I get are always the same—"no f*%#ing way" written all over their faces. Sure, that probably won't make them blend in on base, but it *will* force them to get used to the idea of presenting themselves as nonthreatening. But of course, an unthreatening demeanor doesn't mean they—or you—can't actually *become* a threat, if necessary.

Beyond clothing, ego also drives physical posture, the way you walk, and your general aura. Some walk very confidently. Others walk like they're on a mission. Some walk as if they are superior. All of these traits are driven by ego. They are hard habits to break, but they can be broken through self-discipline. Change your habits, and your ego will follow—and you'll be safer and more capable for it.

So, here it is in a nutshell: you can reduce your threat vulner-abilities through sustained awareness, projection, and demeanor management. That's it.

The Jedburgh teams of yesterday and the clandestine opera-tives of today understand the importance of cultural immer-sion. If you can't do an immersion trip, then research is the next best option. Country studies—researching pertinent country-specific issues, history, politics, culture, threats, and so on—should be undertaken prior to departure. That's what separates the Total Awareness System from the rest—the commitment to studying the environment, its culture, its threats, and consolidating it all into your awareness profile. In Chapter 4, you'll find a series of country guides, broken down by projection and demeanor, that will help you blend in more effectively.

THE COMPONENTS OF PERSONAL AWARENESS

Business casual is a decent disguise that you can wear almost anywhere and it'll be acceptable. A white shirt with a neutral or blue jacket, pants or a knee-length skirt, and dress shoes, that's it. Milan, Kabul, LA, you'll get the same reaction from people—nada. Think about the people you watch at the airport. Now think about the guy you never even noticed, even though you were sitting in the same waiting area with him for four hours. That's the guy you want to be.

The Business Casual Disguise

First, we are going to more fully explore how Personal Awareness—and its specific components, such as physical appearance and actions—can dramatically reduce your visibility, and we'll do that by further breaking down physical appearance/projection and demeanor.

The category of **physical appearance/projection** consists of, but is not limited to: clothing, jewelry, technology, grooming standards, gender, race, and accessories—everything that the general public can observe and judge. Consider this—not many people in the world wear ballcaps, except American men. Look around and see what everyone else is wearing.

I have broken *projection* into *first-*, *second-*, and *third-line gear*, which are terms that I've borrowed from the military.

The terms refer to the layers of gear that a soldier wears into combat. The military would define first-line gear as items required to survive: the clothes you're wearing, a map, compass, first-aid kit, pistol, and so on. Second-line gear would be your fighting gear, which includes your rifle, load-bearing gear, bullets, communication equipment, and night vision goggles. Third-line gear includes your backpack and its contents. Here is how I define these lines of gear in relation to the global traveler and Personal Awareness:

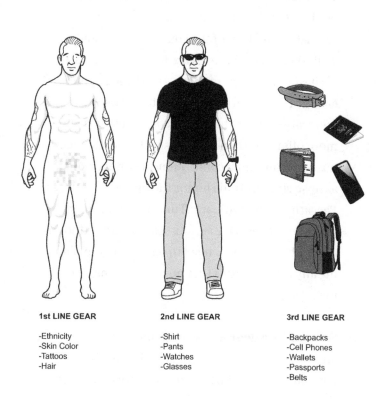

1st LINE GEAR

-Ethnicity
-Skin Color
-Tattoos
-Hair

2nd LINE GEAR

-Shirt
-Pants
-Watches
-Glasses

3rd LINE GEAR

-Backpacks
-Cell Phones
-Wallets
-Passports
-Belts

- **First-line gear** is difficult to change—it's your birthday suit. That's right, the bare-naked truth standing in the mirror looking back at you, waiting for constructive criticism. You want to identify any characteristics that are culturally offensive, would make you stand out in a crowd, or might make you a threat. Specific traits to pay attention to are gender, race, hair color, eye color, skin color, piercings, tattoos, circumcision, and any gross abnormalities. Most of these traits cannot be changed, but all of them must be evaluated against the culture of the country you intend to visit. If racial differences are likely to be an issue, it's best to be aware of them, even though you can't change them. Piercings and tattoos, on the other hand, are choices that you made, and they can be more offensive than you'd suspect. For instance, a nose ring on a man could offend a Hindi woman, as nose rings in India honor the marriage goddess, Parvathi. Iran, Denmark, Turkey, China, and many other countries have serious issues with tattoos. If caught by a wolf, you need to have a story explaining any irregularities that might be offensive or upsetting.

- **Second-line gear** is easy to change—it's anything that touches your skin. Items like hats, sunglasses, shirts, pants, underwear, socks, gloves, necklaces, bracelets, watches, and rings make up a large portion of the physical traits that define a person and may be used to distinguish you from others. Although this is the easiest line of gear to change, most people will not bother. Americans want to look good, smell good, and be noticed. Second-line gear is what provides identity and separates people from one another— which is what you *don't* want to be doing in this case. Loud clothes with logos, brand names, and symbols give rifle sights a place to line up. Subdued second-line gear can make you look like a sheep and help you blend in with the flock.

- **Third-line gear** is anything that touches your clothes. This includes items like jackets, shoes, belts, bags, purses, backpacks, wallets, passports, mobile phones, and laptops. These are items that people use for long periods of time (longevity items) or have in limited quantities when traveling. They make tracking and surveillance easy. (As I mentioned and will continue to discuss, the wolf comes in many forms, and surveillance may be one of them.) Now, I know you've got to take your laptop with you, but keep your third-line gear as minimal and unobtrusive as possible. Don't carry a brightly colored or designer bag. Keep it as common as possible.

Demeanor as a category is defined by your physical actions, including gestures, manners, language, your handshake, your walk, and the way you talk. For this discussion, I have broken demeanor or actions into three major categories: *body language*, *verbal language*, and *protocol*.

- **Body Language** is defined as nonverbal physical movements and expressions that communicate intentional or unintentional thoughts and emotions. A simple, yet powerful body language signal is a person crossing his or her arms. Other than signaling the person is physically cold, this gesture may typically indicate an unconscious barrier has been raised.

- **Verbal Language** is defined as verbal interaction where two or more parties exchange information. Verbal communication includes tone, word choice, and language.

- **Protocol** is defined as international rules and social behavior, which includes body language and communication that are in accordance with a specific culture. Protocol includes greetings, manners, and other actions that conform to a culture norm.

Now that you have the gist of Personal Awareness and the associated terms, you are ready to learn some specifics.

DON'T BE THE UGLY AMERICAN

The term "Ugly American" was most recently introduced to the world by our friends in Hollywood with the movie based on a novel co-written by William Lederer.

The Ugly American was about an ignorant, incompetent American traveling through a fictitious Asian country. In the novel, a Burmese journalist says, "For some reason, the [American] people I meet in my country are not the same as the ones I knew in the United States. A mysterious change seems to come over Americans when they go to a foreign land. They isolate themselves socially. They live pretentiously. They're loud and ostentatious."

Not too far from the truth. The thing is, America as a country tends to be a bit, well, self-centered. We're very caught up in our own little world, and we don't have much of a cultural perspective. Obviously this is a huge generalization, but the outside perspective is that Americans don't have much interest in other cultures and other religions. Now, most Americans will say that we live in the best country in the world—I'm one of them. I've traveled *a lot*, and I feel that way, too. America is great.

But that pride of place can be off-putting when you're overseas, even when it happens totally naturally. Say I'm on the French Riviera and I order some ratatouille and a glass of Bordeaux. Or I *would*, but I'm stuck sitting there for thirty minutes before the waiter manages to come take my order. Americans are used to a very service-oriented life, but not every place is like that. If I'm the only American in that restaurant, I promise you I'm the only one wondering why the service is so goddamn slow. Everyone else is just enjoying the view.

Americans need to learn to treat travel like they are going to a party at the boss's house. You should dress appropriately, eat differently, talk differently, and be respectful to others at the party. Given the recent anti-American sentiment expressed in some countries and groups, you don't want to be the Ugly American!

Some elements of projection and demeanor are entirely out of your control, but that means you should pay very close attention to what *is* within your sphere of influence. Skin color, eye color, and sex are not easily changed. Demeanor, or the way in which you act or carry yourself, however, is just as much a part of you as your race or sex, and some of it cannot be changed. But the small details—your clothing, your accessories, and your actions—are completely controllable.

Jason Bourne knew this lesson all too well. The clandestine assassin navigated his way through third-party surveillance and pursuit in foreign countries with snakelike ease. He moved through train stations, airports, streets, and all of Europe by becoming a sheep. He dressed in muted colors, spoke the language, and became part of his environment. He was, simply, a chameleon.

Most people aren't Jason Bournes. They're Clark W. Griswolds, the fictional character in the National Lampoon movie series. A proud American father, Clark pulled on his favorite "Wally World" sweatshirt, grabbed a Chicago Bears baseball cap, and took his family on vacation to Europe. Most traveling Americans think like Clark: "I'm a proud American, and I'm going to show it."

Although these two fictional characters represent extreme ends of the projection and demeanor trait spectrum, they provide important lessons: be more like Jason, and less like Clark. The following schematic provides a guideline of desirable "Jason" and undesirable "Clark" behaviors.

Jason Bourne   **vs.**   **Clark Griswold**

The accompanying chart provides a quick snapshot of innocent, yet important tip-offs that will draw unwanted attention to you in your world travels. You'll want to work to suppress these common American traits to blend in with the local culture and help ensure secure, safe travel.

The Quintessential "Ugly American"

Identifiers that Signal "The Ugly American"

Asking for Coke	Expensive watches
Asking for ketchup	Wearing athletic shoes
Asking for ice	Wearing flip-flops
Baseball caps	Chewing gum
Sunglasses	Patriotic clothing
High-dollar tech devices	University, college, high-school clothing
Smokeless tobacco	Loud conversations ON YOUR CELLPHONE

There are dozens of additional examples of how Americans inadvertently make themselves stand out and become easy targets. Like the Jedburghs and Griswolds, we all need to learn some new customs to blend in a bit better. It's smart, and it's also good manners.

Let's start with an etiquette lesson.

Etiquette Basics

Etiquette used to mean "keep off the grass." When Louis XIV's gardener at the French court of Versailles discovered that aristocrats were trampling through his gardens, he put signs up, or *etiquettes*, to warn them off. But the dukes and duchesses walked right past them anyway. Finally, the king himself had to decree that no one was to go beyond the bounds of the etiquettes. The term "etiquette" was expanded to mean a ticket to court functions that listed rules on where to stand and what to do. Like language, etiquette evolves, but in a sense, it still means "keep off the grass."

Teaching good manners was considered part of a child's upbringing until the 1960s—public and private schools actually used to include etiquette as part of a well-rounded curriculum. But the liberated '60s and '70s brought a decline in general manners in America. What does this have to do with escaping the wolf? Well, what Americans consider posh or fancy manners are the norm in most countries. We basically eat like slobs in comparison to European-colonized populations.

In business and government arenas today, the term "protocol" is often used instead of etiquette because it sounds more businesslike and official.

"Eating is not an executive skill...but it is especially hard to imagine why anyone negotiating items of importance would consider it possible to skip mastering the very simple requirements...what else did they skip learning?"

—FORTUNE 500 CEO

Noted. You can be the most articulate, well-dressed professional in the room, but if your manners are lacking, especially when dealing with ambassadors and the like, then your true professionalism will be questioned. Let's dig deeper into manners and etiquette to understand how you can use these to blend into the local culture.

Posture at the Table

A. Hands above table
B. Elbows in
C. Straight Back
D. Feet flat on floor

Sit straight, but not stiff, against the back of the chair and rest both feet flat on the ground. Note: you are not straddling the chair, ready to leap out of it and fight someone, and your legs don't need to be spread so wide the people sitting next to you feel cramped.

Elbows should be kept close to your sides when eating, not bowed out exposing your armpits to the world. Move them forward and backward to convey the food to the mouth and to manipulate utensils.

Continental or European standards hold that both hands stay above the table at all times. It is considered rude to have one hand down on your lap and the other above. This custom is centuries-old, dating back to when a hand under the table was considered a threat, indicating that the diner was reaching for a weapon. This is hard for members of the military, who are used to eating fast in tight quarters where it is easier to put one arm under the table.

It should go without saying that in many cultures, nose blowing at the table is considered offensive. Any bodily functions should be taken care of away from the table.

PUTTING IT ALL TOGETHER

I'm not saying you should hide out in your hotel room for fear of not blending in. Of course you'll want to explore this new city, and you should absolutely do so. It's not about locking yourself down and not doing anything—instead, it's about doing your research and knowing where to go, what are the safe places, and how to behave when you're there.

The Total Awareness concept is more than just understanding your environment through your senses. A Total Awareness approach requires you to research and understand the location you are going to encounter. Ask yourself, am I going to a semi-permissive or nonpermissive environment? What threats exist? What do I need to know before I go? We'll discuss those issues in the following chapters. For now, it's important that you understand that the environment drives the awareness layers.

"Travelers never think that they are the foreigners."

—MASON COOLEY

CHAPTER 3 REVIEW

PRACTICE ASSIGNMENT– PERSONAL AWARENESS

WHEN TO NOT BE AN UGLY AMERICAN AND WHEN IT MIGHT BE OKAY

IN THIS CHAPTER, WE'VE EXPLORED HOW TO BLEND IN. IT'S THE LITTLE things that often create cultural challenges when traveling abroad and betray your country of origin—choices in wardrobe, menu selections, and habits that literally shout your national origin.

As discussed, you'll achieve your business objectives and attract less attention from unsavory characters by blending in and taking charge.

PRACTICAL EXAMPLE

- Nonpermissive environment (area with little/no government control)

- Shopping in a town

Good intentions don't always produce good results. I was in Somalia, and I had just finished training twelve Somalis, which was a bit of a challenge given the language barrier. But I was there working with them for weeks, flying in on a CIA bird on a Monday and out again on Friday. I was sleeping in all these different places and staying mobile so I wouldn't get targeted.

We were just wrapping up the mission, and it was time for their final graded exercise—a test of sorts to see if they had learned all they needed to. So the Somali head of intel I was working with, Jamel, and I wandered around the town, shopping, looking around some souks, while the guys we were training carried out surveillance on us. I'd given them encrypted radios and loaded them up with all the gear they would need.

Jamel and I wandered to the first stop, went inside, and checked to see who came in with me, testing them to see if they were following the protocols I'd taught them. This whole time Jamel is chatting with the people in the stores, gesturing at me, but I have no idea what he's saying. Turns out, he thought he would ensure my safety by introducing me to curious locals as a Swedish veterinarian without informing me. Why Swedish? I asked him. "Everyone loves Swedes," he replied.

Now, this put me in kind of a bad spot. I mean, I don't speak Swedish. But we were getting toward the end of the day and the end of the mission, so I rolled my eyes and let it go.

Until that night, when I was sitting in my hotel room, and I got a call on my sat phone, and the guy on the line is yelling at me to get of there, I've got a bunch of crazy people coming to kill me. I didn't know what was going on, but I activated my bug-out plan and ended up at an airstrip in the middle of nowhere. About three hours later, a plane shows up to pick me up. I ask the guys, "What the hell happened?"

Turns out, that night the Arab world went crazy because some Swedish illustrator drew Mohammed—and there I was, apparently Swedish.

So, you know, blending in is just a matter of keeping your mouth shut, your head down, and *not* making stuff up.

STUDY GUIDE QUESTIONS

Why do you think the local population was angry?

What could I have done earlier to change the outcome of this encounter?

STUDY GUIDE ANSWERS

Why do you think the local population was angry?

I had no clue why the local community was up in arms—literally—until I found out the next day that a Swedish cartoonist named Lars Vilks had recently decided to sketch the Prophet Mohammed with the body of a dog, which was taken as a major insult by most of the Islamic world. Talk about bad timing.

What could I have done earlier to change the outcome of this encounter?

LESSONS LEARNED

- Control your guides or liaisons in the country, and have a plan before you go out. In my case, Jamel was trying to be helpful, but no answer is sometimes the best answer.

- That would have been a good trip to be the "Ugly American" versus the "Handsome Swede."

- Don't think that speaking English identifies you as an American. Believe it or not, English truly is the international language. Americans,

Australians, and Brits can usually tell each other apart by accent, but the rest of the broken-English world often cannot tell where you are from.

If direct questions are asked, answer with a broad brush (macro to micro) and flip the conversation back to them. Sample dialogue:

"Where are you from?"

"I am on holiday. Where are you from? How much for the hookah?" Then, control the conversation from there.

Most people, regardless of culture, like to talk about themselves and their culture and provide helpful information. Oh, and of course, try and sell you inflatable Hello Kitty swimming pool rafts (weird, no water or swimming pools for hundreds of miles).

NOTES:

CULTURAL AWARENESS

"If you reject the food, ignore the customs, fear the religion and avoid the people, you might better stay at home."

—JAMES MICHENER

I GREW UP IN SAUDI, LIVING THERE FROM AGE EIGHT UNTIL FOURTEEN. That's a *huge* culture shock for a kid. The minute we got off the plane, they separated the women and children from the men. Going through customs meant a half dozen guys dumping your suitcase on the floor and digging through the pile with sticks. We were bused to a trailer park in the middle of the desert, which would be our temporary housing until we could move onto the compound where the other Americans were. I woke up with a nose full of sand and snot. And that was just my first twelve hours.

Culture combined with the environment it exists in can be shocking. At eight years old, I was appalled. Why were these people like this? But now, having spent the majority of my adult life in Muslim countries, I understand it. The culture isn't wrong, just different. It's what the people who live there know. If we can learn to accept and even embrace it, we can find parallels. Sharing a hookah in the Middle East isn't that different from going outside for a smoke break with your coworkers.

And the thing to remember is, America is a baby compared with the rest of the world. We're the newest culture on the block, while they've been doing their thing for centuries.

You are trying to blend in at micro levels in a foreign country. You may have the wrong skin tone, but at first glance, you don't necessarily have to be American. As discussed in the preceding chapter on Personal Awareness, you can minimize personal traits to call less attention to yourself so you don't stand out as an American. Taking this even further, you can work to blend into the local culture.

CULTURAL AWARENESS

Cultural Awareness (CA) is the assessment and understanding of a specific geographic location's culture, including cultural-specific social protocol and etiquette but going all the way to mannerisms and gestures. As I will continue to stress, it's up to you to take ownership of any journey you embark on.

Using the following list as an outline, take time to learn about the people and culture of your future destinations to increase awareness and make the most of your trip.

1. Country, City

2. Basic History

3. Language

4. Initial Meeting Criteria

5. Dining Protocol

6. Projection

7. Demeanor

8. Business Meeting Criteria

9. Negotiation

10. Special Culture Specifics

Research aside, there are commonalities to practicing Cultural Awareness in any culture you visit.

- Conservative, muted business casual clothing is acceptable in most cultures.

- European table demeanor will work in almost any environment.

Let's take a brief look at some of the subtle, and not so subtle, differences that exist. When it comes to greetings, no, you don't give two kisses to everyone in France, and you don't bow to everyone in an Asian country. The handshake is the correct greeting for someone you're just meeting for the first time, but there are subtle differences.

HANDSHAKING INTELLIGENCE

- **Australia**. Firm grip with two strokes

- **Belgium**. Light pressure and quick stroke

- **China**. Light grip may include pumping, which shows pleasure in the greeting

- **France**. Light grip with a brisk stroke

- **Germany**. Firm grip and one stroke

- **Japan**. Light grip with three or four light strokes

- **Korea**. Medium-firm handshake. To show respect when shaking hands, support your right forearm with your left hand

- **Latin and South America**. Light grip that lingers twice as long as the US handshake

- **Middle East**. Limp and lingering grip with only a slight up-and-down movement, never stroke

- **Sweden**. Firm grip with one brisk stroke

- **US**. Firm, solid grip with two or three strokes

EYE CONTACT INTELLIGENCE

Americans are firm in their belief that good eye contact is important during business and social conversations. In our country, direct eye contact is a sign of openness, honesty, and assertiveness. Averting eye contact can be misconstrued as lack of confidence or deceptive. In many cultures, however, eye contact is avoided.

Consider the following guidelines:

- **South Korea**. Eye contact is important in business and at various other times. It ensures attention, shows sincerity, and forms a subtle but significant bond between individuals.

- **Middle East**. Eye contact is intense. Middle East- erners look intensely into a person's eyes to search their soul and evaluate their inner qualities. They look for dilated pupils to determine true interest in the people they are dealing with.

- **Thailand**. Eye contact is another form of communication by Thais. You can simply make brief eye contact with a waiter or waitress, and they will come to your table.

- **Scandinavia**. Eye contact is appreciated, but far less than that of Americans and British. Swedes look less frequently at their partners but hold their gaze for longer periods of time.

- **Mexico and Puerto Rico.** Direct eye contact is considered an aggressive gesture, so tone it down.

- **Japan**. Eye contact is considered slightly intimidating, so again, don't insist on it.

AMERICAN STYLE OF EATING

American-style eating is what your mom and dad probably taught you, if they taught you at all. I will never forget eating for the first time with a very good friend of mine. He is highly educated, highly intelligent, and culturally savvy. But he held his fork and knife with fists. He buried his face in his plate and went for it, maybe coming up for air a couple of times. At the end, the table was covered in crumbs, meat particles, and spill marks. His mom and dad forgot that lesson, and he was born in the '60s. But if you *were* taught, it would have been something like this:

- The knife is only used for cutting.

- The fork does most of the work and is held in the right hand like a pencil (tines, the points of the fork, are pointed up).

- When cutting, the knife is held with the right hand, and the fork is positioned in the left hand.

- One piece cut at a time.

- Once done cutting, the knife is put on the plate, the fork switched back to the right hand.

- Food is conveyed to the mouth.

That's pretty much what led to the murders of OSS operatives during World War II.

| American Style | Continental Style |

CONTINENTAL STYLE OF EATING

In 1853, a French etiquette book confided that those who wish to eat fashionably should not change their fork from their right hand after they have cut their meat, but raise the meat to their mouth using their left hand. Before long, Europeans of all classes began eating in this way—after all, it's a more efficient way to eat.

The Continental style of eating is becoming more and more popular in the United States, which is handy, because it is a "must" tactic when blending in overseas. Note the differences between Continental and American.

- The knife is held in the right hand for most of the meal and used to help the fork.

- The fork is in the left hand with tines pointed down. The fork is essentially upside down for the entire meal.

- The knife and fork are both held so that your index figures are pointing at the food.

- When cutting, the fork and knife remain in original hands.

- Food is conveyed to the mouth with the tines pointing down.

ASIAN STYLE OF EATING (CHOPSTICKS)

Besides eating the entire meal with chopsticks, there are some interesting points to highlight:

- Never stand or stab your chopsticks into a bowl of rice.

- Never point your chopsticks at someone.

- Do remember to use the large ends of the chopsticks to serve yourself from a community platter.

- Never eat directly from the platter, always place the food on your plate first.

- Don't cross the chopsticks. When not in use, place the chopsticks side by side on the chopstick rest.

- Never place the chopsticks in your mouth—instead, eat the food without touching the chopsticks.

- Slurp your broth with sound.

GENERAL OVERSEAS DINING DOS AND DON'TS

- Do try everything served at least once.

- Do avoid talking with your mouth full.

- Do wait until you are done swallowing before taking a sip of water.

- Do remember solids (food) are always on your left and fluids are on the right.

- Do remember BMW—*bread, meal, water*—in that order from left to right, so that you don't mistakenly use another person's glass or bread plate.

- Do look into the drink, not over it, when drinking.

- Don't overload your plate.

- Don't overload your fork.

- Don't mop your face with the napkin.

- Don't throw your napkin on the dish when done.

- Don't spread your elbows when cutting meat.

- Don't saw the meat.

- Don't chew with your mouth open.

- Don't touch your face or head at the table.

- Don't pick your teeth at the table.

- Don't push your plate away when done.

- Don't gesture with your utensils.

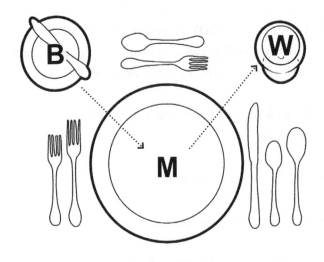

BMW
Bread, Meal, Water

GESTURES

Gestures are a casual, second-class form of communication, but people depend on these subtle movements, postures, actions, and expressions as a shorthand. Like any other form of communication, gestures are culture-specific. A perfectly acceptable gesture in the US may not be appropriate elsewhere.

For example, the "okay" gesture (made by connecting the thumb and forefinger into a circle holding the other three fingers straight) in the US is defined differently around the world:

"Okay" Sign

- **Japan**. Means money...looks like the shape of a coin.

- **France, Belgium, Tunisia**. Worthless or zero.

- **Brazil, Russia, Germany, Turkey, Greece, Malta**. An orifice message.

- **Throughout Europe**. A vague, unspecific obscenity.

The "okay" sign is just one of millions of gestures that can turn a good day bad.

The selected examples highlight dramatically different cultures, attitudes, projection, and demeanor traits. They should help give you a sense of how to research and "project" Cultural Awareness for future destinations.

"Why is it that traveling Americans are always so dreadful?"

—*DODSWORTH* BY SINCLAIR LEWIS

CHAPTER 4 REVIEW

PRACTICE ASSIGNMENT— CULTURAL AWARENESS

IT'S THE LITTLE THINGS THAT COUNT IN CULTURE

IN THIS CHAPTER, WE'VE EXPLORED HOW TO BLEND IN BY STUDYING AND adapting to the local culture. Your advance preparation will be critical in determining the success of your trip.

Every culture has subtle differences. It's important to understand those nuances and not misinterpret them, or create misunderstandings by making an inadvertent mistake that is the result of ignorance. Let's take a look at the challenges presented by a simple dinner invitation.

PRACTICAL EXAMPLE

- Semi-permissive environment (area with some government control)

- Conducting sensitive business negotiations over dinner

You are in China on business and have tried to prepare carefully for these important meetings. In your pre-departure research, you learned that your most senior person should be your spokesperson for the introductory functions. You're a little frustrated with the pace of the meetings, but recognize that it is part of the Chinese culture to take business meetings slowly and to be very process-oriented. You are prepared for the agenda to become a jumping-off point for other discussions. You've taken care to dress conservatively. If you are a man, you are wearing a dark-colored business suit. If you are a woman, you are wearing a conservative business suit or dress with a high neckline and flat shoes (or shoes with very low heels). You are avoiding bright colors.

You have been invited to dinner in the home of one of the Chinese business owners and are having trouble deciding what type of gift to bring for the hostess. You recognize this is an important gesture, and you're nervous about the local cultural protocol around gift giving and dining.

STUDY GUIDE QUESTIONS

What sort of gift would be appropriate and what color gift wrap should be avoided?

What should you do when you arrive and what sort of dining manners are important?

STUDY GUIDE ANSWERS

What sort of gift would be appropriate and what color gift wrap should be avoided?

Being invited to the home of a Chinese person is a great honor. The Chinese prefer to entertain in public places rather than in their homes, especially when entertaining foreigners. You should absolutely bring a small gift for the hostess.

In general, gifts are given at Chinese New Year, weddings, births, and more recently (because of marketing) birthdays. The Chinese like food, so a nice food basket will make a great gift. Avoid gifts of scissors, knives, or other cutting utensils as they indicate the severing of the relationship. Also avoid clocks, handkerchiefs, or straw sandals as they are associated with funerals and death. Do not bring flowers, as many Chinese associate these with funerals. Do not wrap gifts in white, blue, or black paper. Four is an unlucky number, so do not give four of anything. Eight is the luckiest number, so giving eight of something brings luck to the recipient. Always present gifts with two hands, and understand that gifts will not be opened when received. Gifts may also be refused three times before they are accepted.

What should you do when you arrive and what sort of dining manners are important?

Learn to use chopsticks and be sure to arrive on time. Remove your shoes before entering the house, and wait to be told where to sit. The guest of honor will be given a seat facing the door. The host begins eating first and offers the first toast. Try everything that is offered to you, and never eat the last piece from the serving tray. Be observant of the needs of others. Return chopsticks to rest after every few bites and when you drink or stop to speak. Do not put bones in your bowl. Place them on the table or in a special bowl reserved for that purpose. Lift the rice bowl and hold it close to your mouth while eating. Do not be offended if a Chinese person makes slurping or belching sounds—these merely indicate enjoyment of the food. There are no strict rules about finishing all the food in your bowl, but eat well to demonstrate that you are enjoying the meal.

None of this is specific to Chinese culture. I mean, it's not like Chinese people are particularly sensitive! You want to be aware of the cultural meaning behind your actions and the actions of others wherever you go.

Sometimes there's a religious aspect. If I'm sitting on a bus in a Muslim country, I might be uncomfortable and want to cross my ankle over the other leg. For me, that's just because I've been sitting for hours. But for them, showing the sole of your shoe is disrespectful.

It might also be about hygiene. In most Middle Eastern countries, you eat with the right hand and only the right hand—and you definitely don't go back and forth between the two. This is a leftover from nomadic culture, when one hand was used for eating, and the other hand was used for hygiene. Culturally, that's how they kept from getting sick. So if you're sharing a meal, make sure you follow their example and use the correct hand.

Say you want to give a gift to a Japanese businessperson that you want to broker a deal with, and you bring them this really cool watch. Nice present, right? But not in Japan. In Japan, a clock represents the time someone's going to die, and it's not something you want to wear all the time.

The reality is that getting any of these situations wrong is extremely unlikely to result in someone screaming at you and putting you in any kind of danger. However, a best case scenario is they're thinking, "Yeah, all right American, nice try," when what you're going for is "Wow, what a thoughtful gift. This person really thinks things through, and that's someone I'd like to be in business with."

NOTES:

_____

_____

_____

_____

_____

_____

_____

_____

_____

_____

_____

_____

_____

_____

_____

THIRD-PARTY AWARENESS

DETERMINING THIRD-PARTY AWARENESS THROUGH TRAVELCRAFT

"When you travel, remember that a foreign country is not designed to make you comfortable. It is designed to make its own people comfortable."

—CLIFTON FADIMAN

THIRD-PARTY AWARENESS (3PA) IS THE GENERAL PUBLIC'S PERCEPTION of you and your actions—in this case, that includes citizens of the country in which you are traveling, law enforcement, criminals, or even a terrorist residing in or visiting the host country. As mentioned in Chapter 1, you cannot totally control the perceptions and judgments of others. To reduce Third-Party Awareness, you need to blend into the environment using your Personal Awareness (the image and demeanor you project) and Situational Awareness skillsets.

Increased Personal Awareness plus increased Situational Awareness equals decreased Third-Party Awareness.

TRAVELCRAFT

You can determine who is scrutinizing you and your every movement through the use of *travelcraft techniques*. A travelcraft repertoire will help you assess whether you are under physical or technical surveillance. The spy world would call this tradecraft, but just to be clear, you don't want the wolf to think you're a spy. Trust me, you don't want the kind of attention that would produce. The techniques you'll be using are non-alerting, allowing you to decrease your footprint without tipping anyone off to the fact that you think something is amiss. They are not designed to "bust" the bad guy or alert the surveillance team, but instead to increase your awareness, make you more confident as you transition through your Modes of Awareness cycle, and enable you to escape the wolf in a discreet manner.

The first phase of any criminal or terror attack is information collection. The bad guys want to know where you are staying, where you work, your modes of transportation, the routes you walk and drive, where you dine, and who you dine with. In short, they want to know everything, and all of this information will be used to determine your "pattern of life"—a study of your daily, weekly, and monthly activities. Once your "pattern of life" is analyzed, the crook or terrorist determines the vulnerabilities that set you up for attack, exploitation, and/or kidnapping scenarios.

The first weapon in their arsenal is your routine, and so your first line of defense is varying or shifting that routine. If your routine is always changing, it will keep potential threats off balance and make it difficult to target you. Break down your routines into three dimensions—time, routes, and destinations. These must all be altered on a regular basis. The times you travel, the routes you walk or drive, and the places you go will determine their attack points. Constantly changing those points will make targeting you difficult.

Timelines, routes, and destinations are collected by both technical and physical surveillance. That means before we discuss defensive and detection techniques, you must gain a broader understanding of how surveillance works.

Surveillance is an assessment of vulnerabilities in an attempt to determine any information available, from any source, about you or your activities that can be used against you. If you recognize that you are under surveillance, then you can take preventive measures that will hopefully deter further interest. You won't be able to determine whether the surveillants are intelligence agents or terrorists, so you will need to be discreet in order to avoid tipping off those you suspect of watching you. Again, to be clear: don't let them know you know. Don't confront them. That will *not* increase your chances of safely escaping the wolf.

The subject of surveillance is extremely important to anyone conducting business abroad, as a traveler could be under surveillance for any number of reasons. Monitoring doesn't necessarily need to be conducted by foreign intelligence or a security service. Terrorists and criminals also use surveillance to plan their attacks, though honestly, you're unlikely to be a target for terrorists—or at least, not you specifically. If you are attacked by terrorists, it'll be because you were in the wrong place at the wrong time. On the other hand, business travelers have a much higher likelihood of being targeted by criminals or someone engaging in corporate espionage, and surveillance by one of those is something you should absolutely be on the lookout for.

I've had lots of experience with surveillance, from both sides— I've been the one who was watched, and the one doing the watching. Now, the work I was doing meant that I needed to behave in a certain way to achieve my objective, and I'm going to give you an example to help you understand how surveillance works and why—but this is definitely not intended as a story to emulate. Remember, we're trying to escape the wolf.

At the time, though, I was trying to draw them in. I was on the trail of a terrorist with connections between Somalia, Yemen, and Pakistan. I knew that he was going to be leaving Somalia on a big dhow (a type of sailing vessel common in the Red Sea), and I wanted to be able to track him. I flew into Oman, knowing that I was going to be under surveillance from the moment I landed.

Obviously this was a conundrum. I needed to lose my surveillance in order to do what I'd come here to do. But here's what I'd learned—the best way to lose your surveillance is to make them so bored they stop doing their job well. Like I said, I've been on both sides, and most of the time surveillance is mind-numbingly boring. That's something I could take advantage of.

I spent a couple of days at my hotel, taking the time to set a pattern of life. I worked out, did some tourist stuff, and went to the Starbucks. I did the same goddamn predictable thing every day. For you, this would be really stupid—it would make you easy to track. You should maintain an irregular pattern of life that would keep people off balance and make them decide you're not worth the trouble, and move onto someone else who has the perfect routine—someone easier to exploit.

Colonization plays a big role in understanding what a country's tactics will be. I knew that these guys had been trained by the Brits, which meant they were going to be pretty good. If they even suspected who I was or what I might be doing, I wasn't going to be able to lose them through an irregular pattern of life. So I needed to lose them another way.

In order to track that dhow, I needed to make it to the fishing village where it was going to be—without making the guys tailing me suspicious. I assumed (as you should) that everyone in my hotel was reporting to foreign intel. So I went up to the concierge and asked, "Hey, where's there a cool place to see the shoreline, maybe go fishing?" Of course, I already knew that the closest place was that same village, but I wanted to establish a reason for going there.

In surveillance, density determines distance, and vice versa. If you're in a dense area, like an urban environment, then your surveillance has to stay close; otherwise they'll lose you. Red lights, crowds, etc.—all of that makes it hard to tail somebody unless you're nearby. On the other hand, if there's no density, surveillance can stay pretty far away, which will allow them to track the person but be less noticeable.

Unless of course they're the only other people around. On that drive out to the fishing village, I was headed south for three hours on a big empty road, and the whole time there's a car a mile or so behind me. Which is weird, right? Ordinarily a car would turn, and even if it's going to the same place, it would either catch up to me or I'd lose it. Normal people out for a drive don't stay precisely a mile back.

So yeah, I knew they were there. Once we got closer to the village, they had to come in close again to keep track of me— so all of a sudden that Corolla that was way back is now close enough for me to get its make, model, and license plate. And would you believe it, that was the same car I saw while I was out running yesterday. What are the odds?

Coincidence doesn't exist. If you can confirm the same person, or the same make and model car, in a different zip code, you're definitely under surveillance.

But I couldn't be sure that Corolla was it for my surveillance. They might have had someone already down there at the fishing village. So I had to keep playing it safe. I established a new pattern of life, and it was just as boring as before. I scheduled a fishing trip. I did some jet skiing. I went to a café (no Starbucks down there). I worked out. I used the same door in and out of the hotel every time, and always went to bed at a reasonable hour.

And then, after a few days of this, I broke my pattern. I knew exactly where they'd be watching, so I left my hotel by a different exit. I'd already scouted my target boat while I was renting the jet ski, so I could move quickly. I planted the tracking device and got out of there. For the next few days, I continued that boring pattern of life. I even went on that fishing trip—caught a few good ones, too. Then I went back up to Oman, spent a few more days playing tourist, and finally got out of there.

Again, this is what you *don't* want to do. The point of this story is to help you understand the predator-prey philosophy of surveillance. I was setting myself up as easy prey. Don't do that. Be someone who is way too much of a pain in the ass to track.

TYPES OF SURVEILLANCE

Surveillance takes many forms. An observer can be physically or electronically watching or monitoring your activities in your hotel room or office. Or you can be subject to mobile surveillance by being followed on foot or by a vehicle. ***Physical***

Surveillance consists of an individual or group of individuals physically following, observing, and tracking every movement of a target. *Technical Surveillance* consists of following, observing, and tracking a target with electronic equipment.

Anatomy of Physical Surveillance

Active Surveillance (short-term). Aggressive surveillance with an emphasis on actual 24/7 eyes-on surveillance. A trained surveillance team may employ this tactic pre-attack, pre-capture, or pre-arrest. An untrained team may employ this technique and compromise themselves early due to overly aggressive tactics. Active surveillance consists of constant foot and mobile shadowing of the target by single or multiple surveillant(s) with hourly activity. It's not easy to do without being spotted—if you're paying attention.

Passive Surveillance (long-term). Loose, progressive surveillance with an emphasis on long-term, limited exposure to the target. A trained or untrained surveillance team may use this type of surveillance during an initial pattern-of-life analysis or when discretion is paramount. Passive surveillance would consist of *static* surveillance by single or multiple surveillant(s) staged at particular points of interest (e.g., home or work). Typically, no actual following of the target takes place.

Physical surveillance is an art, and it takes a considerable amount of training for a team to be effective. For this reason, criminals or terrorists are considered sloppy and easy to spot. If you understand surveillance and use the Total Awareness System, amateur tactics will stand out. There are countless ways to conduct active and passive surveillance. I will briefly describe the most common.

Static Surveillance

Mobile Surveillance

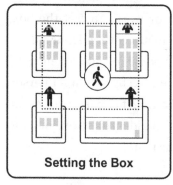

Setting the Box

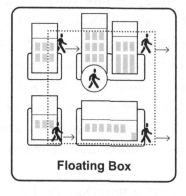

Floating Box

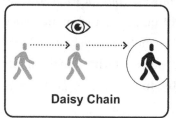

Daisy Chain

Anatomy of Physical Surveillance

Static Surveillance. Also known as *fixed surveillance*, this method consists of observing the target at a specific location from a fixed position. Static surveillance can be conducted from any location near or around the target person's residence, office, or hotel.

Mobile Surveillance. Also known as *the follow*, this consists of observing the target while traveling or moving on foot and/ or in a vehicle. Mobile surveillance collects information that cannot be collected by static surveillance.

Static and mobile surveillance can also be used concurrently to enhance the effectiveness of an operation.

Setting the Box. Most surveillance teams "pick up" a target from a static location like home or work. To "set the box," multimember, static surveillance teams cover all four sides of a structure. Each member covers possible exit and entrance points for the side of the structure used by the target person. A team member who observes the target departing or entering the structure will report a positive identification, location, dress, and activity to the rest of the team.

Floating Box. Once the target moves from location to location, the surveillance team might employ a technique called a "floating box." The multimember mobile surveillance "box" will discreetly surround the target person during foot or mobile movement. Each member rotates in and out of position to maintain constant observation. This technique is very difficult for a team to perfect and employ. Risk of compromise is high.

Daisy Chain. A daisy chain can be used instead of a floating box to decrease possible compromise. A passive and static multimember linear surveillance model, it involves individual surveillants staged along a target's known route. The surveillants are typically ahead of the target, observing and reporting the target's arrival and departure at specific locations along the route.

These are just a few of the tactics that could be employed against you during your travels.

Physical Surveillance Recognition

As mentioned, almost every criminal act, from a purse snatching to a terrorist bombing, involves some degree of pre-operational surveillance. They will always check you out, at least for a little while, before attacking. And while they are observing you, they become vulnerable to detection. Why? Because criminals, even militants planning terrorist attacks, often become quite sloppy when they are casing their intended targets. They have been able to get away with their careless tactics for so long because, sheep-like, most people simply do not pay attention. On a positive note, these shoddy practices will stand out to the totally aware sheepdog.

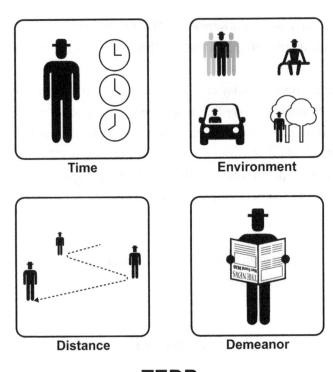

Time

Environment

Distance

Demeanor

TEDD

There are several ways to confirm surveillance, one of which goes by the acronym TEDD, for *Time, Environment, Distance,* and *Demeanor.* In other words, surveillance can be assumed if you see someone repeatedly over *time,* in different *environments,* and over *distance*; a conspicuous display of poor *demeanor* is another sign that you might be under surveillance.

By poor demeanor, I mean that a person is *acting* unnaturally. This behavior can look blatantly suspicious. It might look like a person who is lurking around or has no reason for being where he is or for doing what he is doing. In movies, this will look like someone reading a newspaper upside down or trying on sunglasses for way too long. Sometimes, however, poor demeanor can be subtler, and can just be something you sense on instinct, rather than something you observe that you can put words to. Other giveaways include moving when the target moves, communicating when the target moves, avoiding eye contact with the target, making sudden turns or stops, or even using hand signals to communicate with other members of a surveillance team.

In the terrorism realm, exhibiting poor projection can also include wearing unseasonably warm clothing, such as trench coats in the summer; displaying odd bulges under clothing or wires protruding from clothing; unnaturally sweating, mumbling, or fidgeting; or attempting to avoid security personnel. In addition, according to some reports, suicide bombers often exhibit an intense stare as they approach the final stages of their mission. They seem to have tunnel vision, being able to focus only on their intended target.

If you are a specific target of a planned attack, you may be able to use time, environment, and distance to track TEDD, but if the subway car you are riding in or the building where you work is the target, you might only have the element of demeanor to key on. This is also true in the case of criminals who behave like "ambush predators" and lurk in an area waiting for a victim. Because their attack cycle is extremely condensed, the most important element to watch for is demeanor. Are you sick of hearing how important demeanor is yet?

The Modes of Awareness cycle will help you recognize odd behaviors, unnatural posturing, and suspicious acts. TEDD will enhance the decision and action arm of the OODA loop, for it can be used not only to confirm surveillance but also to identify general criminal threats. There is, however, no single technique that can confirm or deny surveillance. Knowing the environment prior to departure, understanding the threats within the environment, and employing a Total Awareness approach at all times will ensure that you have a good chance of detecting surveillance and its eventual consequences.

How to Confirm that You Are Under Physical Surveillance

Targeting

If you are traveling abroad on business, you could be targeted by an intelligence agency, a security service, or for that matter, a competitor, should you have knowledge of or be carrying sensitive or proprietary information. Certain indicators or situations are red flags, signaling unwarranted interest in your activities. These situations should be closely scrutinized and avoided, if at all possible. A few of the most common scenarios used by intelligence/security services, all of which have resulted in successful acquisition of information from the targeted individual, are listed below:

- Repeated contact with a local or third-country national who is not involved in your business interests or the purpose of your visit, but appears at each function as a result of invitations to social or business functions. If you see the same person repeatedly, pay attention to their demeanor to see if they appear to have more than just a passing interest in you and your business activities.

- A foreign national of a hostile host government; someone that, for business reasons, you must have frequent contact with and/or maintain a close relationship with. In these instances, be cautious and do not allow the relationship to develop any further than at a strictly business level.

- An accidental encounter with a local national who seems just a bit too friendly. Be suspicious of any unknown local national who strikes up a conversation and wants to:

  * Practice English or another language

  * Talk about your country of origin or your employment

* Buy you a drink because he or she has taken a liking to you

* Talk to you about politics

* Use myriad other excuses to begin a "friendly" relationship

- If any of the above or anything else occurs that just does not feel right, BE SUSPICIOUS! Such a scenario may be innocent, but it won't hurt to exercise prudence and good judgment. Trust your instincts.

- If you have any reason to believe that you are being targeted by an intelligence or security service or terrorist group, there is only one course of action to follow: report your suspicions to the affiliate, embassy, or consulate and follow their guidance.

Anatomy of Technical Surveillance

Technical Surveillance is the following, observing, and tracking of a target using electronic equipment—i.e., a bug. The success of audio technical surveillance depends directly on human failure. So, I want to discuss the importance of communication security. Let's face it, if you were able to keep your mouth shut, concealed audio devices wouldn't be a threat. Big mouths coupled with big egos lead to nothing but big trouble. Here is an example.

In a live broadcast from the Iraqi desert, journalist Geraldo Rivera instructed his photographer to tilt the camera down to the sand in front of his feet so that he could draw a map. Rivera then outlined a map of Iraq and showed the relative location of Baghdad and his location with the Army's 101st Airborne unit. The reporter then continued with his diagram to illustrate where the 101st would be going next. Big news for everyone back home, sure, but he compromised the operation he was with, therefore compromising the success of the war and the lives of soldiers.

This is a very extreme example of what *not* to do, but it highlights how valuable information can be, and how important it is to use common sense and discretion.

As always, personal awareness is key to successfully eluding technical hits. Your projection and demeanor must remain consistent with your surroundings. Once again, if you're being watched, give them nothing to look for and nothing to glean information from. If you're being listened to, give them nothing to hear. If you're being followed, give them nothing to see.

Loose Lips Sink Ships

Millions of people volunteered or were drafted for military duty during World War II. The majority of these citizen-soldiers had no idea how to conduct themselves to prevent inadvertent disclosure of important information to the enemy. To remedy this, the government established rules of conduct. The following is excerpted from a document given to each soldier as he entered the battle area.

COMSEC–Communication Security is a process by which a group or individual can deny adversaries information about intentions by identifying, controlling, and protecting evidence of the planning and execution of travel.

- Don't write military information of Army units–their location, strength, material, or equipment.

- Don't write of military installations.

- Don't write of transportation facilities.

- Don't write of convoys, their routes, ports (including ports of embarkation and disembarkation), time en route, naval protection, or war incidents occurring en route.

• Don't disclose movements of ships, naval or merchant, troops, or aircraft.

• Don't mention plans, forecasts, or orders for future operations, whether known or just your guess.

• Don't write about the effect of enemy operations.

• Don't tell of any casualty until released by proper authority (the Adjutant General) and then only by using the full name of the casualty.

• Don't attempt to formulate or use a code system, cipher, or shorthand, or any other means to conceal the true meaning of your letter. Violations of this regulation will result in severe punishment.

• Don't give your location in any way except as authorized by proper authority. Be sure nothing you write about discloses a more specific location than the one authorized.

During World War II, all they had to worry about were handwritten blunders. Today, with technology-driven communication, these same blunders can be made via multiple mediums, delivering the information instantly. Emails, phone conversations, texting, chat rooms, and more are areas of vulnerability. *Discipline and discretion are instrumental in preventing communication compromise.*

Technical Surveillance Recognition

On a positive note, most technical surveillance mechanisms require some kind of installation. Installation requires humans, humans with limited time whose stress responses can cause notable mistakes. Signs of these mistakes can indicate possible technical attacks within your hotel room, rental car, or office space. Fortunately, with some work on your part, you may be able to detect these signs.

INTRUSION DETECTION

Intrusion detection techniques are meant to alert you to possible entry, not to bust the bad guy. Intrusion detection techniques—also known as traps, personal countermeasures, or physical countermeasures—have been around for centuries, ever since sailors and pirates used thief knots (which look exactly like square knots) to tie up and secure their personal ditty bags. The intrusion detection technique was the knot itself. If a curious or thieving sailor or pirate were to open the ditty bag to view its contents without paying attention to the knot, they would naturally tie a square knot upon closure of the bag. Although the knots look similar, they are in fact very different. With that simple measure, the owner of the ditty bag would know that someone had been invading his privacy.

It's important that any intrusion detection technique you use be as natural and easy to remember as the thief knot. Beyond that it should also be subtle. You do not want to set obvious traps, which may bring on even more scrutiny by the invaders. There is no right or wrong technique as long as it's creative, natural to the environment, discreet, and easy to remember. Here are two methods to consider:

1. **Cardinal Bearings**. Place an item on a north, east, south, or west alignment. For example, set a bottle of water near the USB ports of your laptop in your hotel room, and point any letter on the label of the water bottle "north." Place it so that the bottle must be moved in order to access the USB port. If the label is not aligned upon your return, you can assume attack. Similarly, you can hang the "do not disturb" sign on your doorknob so that a disruption

of cardinal alignment betrays any unauthorized room entry—never fall prey to the assumption that a "do not disturb" sign will truly keep maids or other hotel employees out.

A

Coffee has been placed blocking USB ports. Label is facing North.

B

Coffee has been moved presumably to access USB ports. Label is now facing West.

Cardinal Bearings

1. **Discreet Alignment**. Discreet alignment is the alignment of any object that has the potential for scrutiny or exploitation (e.g., a laptop, briefcase, documents, or luggage) with another object or part of the room. For example, you could place a closed folder of documents on a desk and align or point the right corner at the alarm clock on the nightstand. Once again, if the corner of the folder is not pointed precisely at the alarm clock upon your return, it is safe to assume intrusion.

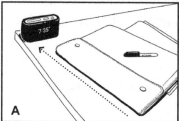
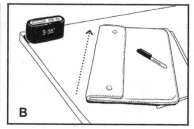

Laptop Case is pointed towards alarm clock.   Laptop case has been moved, now pointing away from alarm clock.

Discreet Alignment

These techniques are limited only by your imagination and the environment. They can be used in your hotel room, office, and rental car.

Hotel Rooms

Always assume that host nation government agencies have access to your room and are perfectly capable of conducting a room "toss," or search, if they so desire. An overt search will result in noticeable physical movement of items in the room. But a properly conducted covert search leaves no signs that a search took place at all. Government agencies will tend to have management open doors for them rather than break in clandestinely, which means that they will leave no signs of forced entry in their stead. On the other hand, criminals or terrorists will not have the same luxury and will often leave behind telltale signs of a clandestine break-in. In either case, however, signs of a covert search can be detected via a series of careful checks and balances.

Upon entering the hotel room for the first time, take a mental snapshot of the room. Set a mental baseline by noting the following:

- The general condition of the door, door jam, and door surface

- The floor directly under and around power outlets, phone outlets, air vents, and other electronics (common technical installation points)

- How clean or dirty those areas are and any displacement of the carpet in and around those areas

- Whether the windows are locked or unlocked and whether access points from balconies, ladders, or other vantage points could be used to enter your room

- The cleanliness of the windowsills

Remember, the room may have already been "hit," so don't do anything that would alert anyone who might be monitoring you. This checklist can be performed on an initial walk-through of the hotel room, while retaining a relaxed, discreet manner.

Once you've set your mental baseline, it will be much easier to notice any changes or discrepancies. Each time you re-enter the room, note any changes—scarring or chipped paint in and around the door-locking mechanisms, door jam, and strike plates. Note any additional sheetrock particles, dust, paint chips, wiring, or other signs of installation in and around power outlets, phone outlets, air vents, and other electronics within the room. By paying attention and using intrusion detection techniques, you will enhance your ability to detect possible technical attacks. In any case, good projection and demeanor will prove the installs worthless to those trying to collect information about you or your company.

Rental Cars

Rental cars are no different than hotel rooms—except for the fact that a rental car is actually more likely to be "hit" than a hotel room. All in all, vehicles are easy targets for technical attacks. They are easy to break into and, due to their small size, easy to bug with a quick installation. They have built-in batteries that can power installed devices. Vehicles are usually left alone all night, and they are prime places for mobile phone conversations. (Most people feel comfortable talking about anything once "safely" inside a vehicle.)

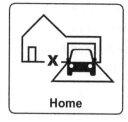
Home

Parking Lot

Parking Garage

Common Attack Points

Fortunately, personal awareness can eliminate this threat completely. Here are some tips to help you identify technical monitoring installations in a vehicle:

- Keep rental vehicles soiled. Note the displacement patterns of dirt around windows and doors. This will make it easier to identify possible entry. It's hard for bad guys to replace dust and dirt and make it look natural.

- Pay attention to preexisting soiled areas on the hood and its margins. The soiled areas could be cleaned along with the bad guy's fingerprints.

- With clean vehicles, pay attention to existing smudge marks, handprints, and weather stripping.

- Pay particular attention to the passenger side of a vehicle. A trained entry specialist will always enter through entry points opposite of the driver.

- Removal of floor mats makes cleanup more difficult for the bad guy. Any debris he has left cannot be simply dumped from the floor mat into a bag. He will actually have to pick it up off the floor and out of the carpet, likely leaving particles behind.

- Examine the interior dash, stereo, air conditioning, and accessory plastic housings and moldings for scars, scratches, and misalignment. Removal of plastic parts with metal screwdrivers can leave scarring.

- Look for wire, wire insulation, and metal and plastic filings on floorboards, floor mats, and outside entry points.

- As for your parking choice: the more public, the better.

Other Technical Ruses

A surveillance team can introduce a technical device by means of a "Trojan Horse," a technique coined in honor of the way the Greeks famously gained entry to the city of Troy during the Trojan War by building a massive, hollow wooden horse and hiding a group of elite Greek soldiers inside. The Greeks delivered the horse to the front gate of Troy and pretended to sail away. Thinking the horse an admission of defeat and a gift to the victors by the Greeks, the Trojans pulled the giant wooden horse within the city walls and celebrated their triumph and unwittingly brought the Greek soldiers inside their city.

Ever since, the Trojan Horse has been a valued trick used by many people, groups, and governments. Today, a technical device delivered right to your hotel room can work in much the same manner. So beware of random deliveries of welcome gifts, promotional items, and any other products that could conceal a technical device.

One surprisingly common technique is to leave a removable computer USB flash drive on the ground of a company parking lot. You (or rather, the sheep version of you) innocently come along and think you've scored a free flash drive. You pop it into your computer, and the device silently steals company data and sends back a signal to an offsite thief.

Along those same lines, a technical device can be installed on items that you must check or store for short periods of time. For example, if you go to a restaurant and check your coat, a device could be installed while you dine. If you allow a hotel bellboy to take your luggage to your room, your luggage could be vulnerable to technical hits. These kinds of methods are virtually unlimited, so always be suspicious of Trojan Horse installations, and never let anything important leave your sight.

ANTI-SURVEILLANCE OR "ESCAPE"

Anti-surveillance measures consist of actions taken to elude or escape a possible surveillance team. You can employ anti-surveillance techniques regardless of whether surveillance is actually detected. If you are like me and assume you are being followed at all times, anti-surveillance may be the tool of choice, but the goal is to successfully employ it without the surveillance team realizing it. Remember, it's best to be a sheepdog in sheep's clothing. An easy way to do so is to set up the surveillance team for failure from the very beginning.

One anti-surveillance tactic is the creation of an "accordion effect" that spreads out the surveillance team beyond recovery and forces them to lose sight of you. An easy way to do this is by driving from congested areas to non-congested areas and back. For example, driving through a downtown environment with lots of traffic lights, jumping onto a highway, and then exiting into another congested area will naturally cause the surveillance to get stretched out. Remember, "density determines distance." If a team gets into a dense or congested area, they will tactically close up the distance between themselves and their target; in a rural area, the team will increase the distance between themselves and the target. By going back and forth between the two environments, you will essentially use this rule against them. Ultimately, creativity always wins, whether you're the target or the surveillance team. So make sure you're always more creative than the adversary.

Most anti-surveillance tactics can be used on foot, but will be more difficult to perform discreetly. In a car, you can speed up and slow down, use your mirrors, and go varying distances from point to point. When you're on foot, you can't start running, constantly looking back, or hiding in the bushes, unless you want to really elevate Third-Party Awareness. What you *can* do is use public transportation, congested shopping malls, and multilevel buildings to lose surveillance. Getting "lost" in density is a great way to make the surveillance team think that they lost you, versus thinking that *you* lost *them*. Anti-surveillance tactics are endless, but employing them properly and discreetly is the difficult part.

The "X" Factor and The Ambush

If your surveillance determines that you are onto them, they may try to capture you. If you use the Total Awareness System, getting caught is preventable, but as mentioned, no system is 100 percent foolproof. Sometimes things do go wrong.

If someone does try to capture you, there are some tactics and techniques you can use to escape. The first, and simplest, is to sidestep the threat of capture by avoiding what I call the "X" factor.

The "X" is an invisible zone where your adversary or attacker might decide to ambush you. Your attacker decides the location along your route where you are most vulnerable or distracted and then strikes with lightning speed, hoping to catch you totally unaware. The chosen location is intended to provide the attacker the greatest possibility of success with the least amount of attention from third parties. Remember, most bad guys don't want to get caught, so that limits their option to Xs that are not surrounded by curious bystanders, law enforcement, or witnesses. The X can be an area where you are driving, walking, sitting, or working.

The X doesn't have to be a particular spot on the ground. Potential ambush scenarios aren't like a Roadrunner and Coyote cartoon. There's no big block letter X marking the spot where the Coyote intends to roll the boulder down on the Roadrunner. Remember the attempted action against me in

Africa? The X was somewhere between the motorcycle-borne surveillant and the two cars pretending to be broken down. That's a decent-sized X-zone.

As you use your Modes of Awareness cycle more often, you will start to identify possible Xs. And once you start identifying Xs, mentally running through reaction scenarios for them will better prepare you for possible attack. Practicing this over time will ultimately put you ahead of any adversary, no matter how much preparation he puts into his attack.

Practical Travel Example

I got ambushed in Iraq. My team had pulled into a big Marine perimeter. They'd placed artillery and light, armored vehicles in a circle a few miles in diameter.

Seems like that'd be a safe zone, right? It's pretty much like making it back to your hotel room and figuring you can relax. And we did. We let our guard down. But your hotel room can be the X. In this case, that perimeter was the X. Never assume that where you settle is actually safe.

We'd been up for five days straight, and were so relieved to be protected by these badass Marine, light, reconnaissance vehicles. They're wheeled tanks, basically. I told my guys to loosen their gear and climb underneath some vehicles to get some sleep. I volunteered to take first watch. So I was sitting there with my night vision goggles on, and I saw movement in some vegetation about fifty yards away. Honestly, I figured it was a Marine who couldn't be bothered to go to the latrine. But I kept an eye on it—and good thing, too, because after a minute, a guy stood up holding an AK-47. That's a distinct-looking weapon, and you know it when you see it.

I quietly called it out, letting my guys know about the threat, but there was no way to do that without being heard. Immediately I started receiving gunfire, and I was out in the open with no cover. I hit the deck and yelled to my guys to start shooting, which they did.

It turns out the Marines had made that big perimeter without really clearing it. They assumed it was empty, but that guy with the AK-47 was there the whole time, just chilling in the bushes waiting for his moment. If I hadn't spotted him, he'd have come to kill as many of us as he could while we slept.

Even the safest place can be an X. You've got to stay wary and keep your personal awareness high at all times.

Anatomy of an Ambush

The ambush is a long-established military tactic in which the attacker uses concealment to attack a moving or stationary target. Ambushes have consistently been used in warfare throughout history, but have also been adopted by petty thieves, kidnappers, and terrorists. Attackers strike from concealed positions within dense underbrush, behind hill-tops, behind buildings, and around any corner or alley in the world. There are three fundamental parts to an ambush to ensure success—*speed, stealth,* and *surprise.*

1. **Speed.** The attacker doesn't want to spend any more time than necessary in or around the X. The attacker wants the action against you to be quick and effective, leaving little time for reaction. The planned action is going to be executed as fast as possible to prevent detection, and to decrease reaction time by you and third parties. Bottom line, time is very valuable to the attacker, and that's something we can take advantage of. If we increase our speed, we decrease the effectiveness of the attacker's plan, because now his timing is off. Moving fast through possible Xs and moving fast while under attack will greatly handicap the attacker.

2. **Stealth.** The attacker needs to hide or conceal himself until the right moment. His concealment must be invisible to you and not look suspicious to third parties. Concealment points must allow the attacker to observe you without detection while providing easy access to you during the attack. There are a lot of variables to being stealthy that limit the options of attack, making the location of

possible Xs limited as well. If we know the attacker must hide from us, yet still observe us and have access to us for the attack, we have a better sense of where to look for him and identify him prior to attack. The Modes of Awareness cycle will help you sift through possible Xs and concealment locations.

3. **Surprise**. The attacker wants to catch you completely off guard and paralyze you. He wants to strike fear into you, so much so that you make little or no response. He does not want a fight, and the best way to avoid one is by catching you by surprise. Running mental "what if" scenarios with possible courses of action will help to diffuse the element of surprise when it occurs. You can use your Modes of Awareness cycle to factor in the element of surprise and move from Alert Mode to Crisis Mode. Then, use your OODA loop to help transition your way back to Pre-Crisis. Having this system in place will exponentially increase your survivability.

The goal within any human-versus-human encounter is to prevail and survive. As mentioned in prior chapters, you want to limit exposure to the threat and increase survivability. To do this, you must have the proper mental tools (Modes of Awareness cycle), tactics (travelcraft techniques), and skill (constant use of both).

Practical Travel Example

Consider this simple scenario. You are walking down a scary alley at night and are confronted by a bum hiding behind a trash can. The bum is focused only on you and begins the attack (action). You begin OODA loop: you *Observe* the threat, you *Orient* to the threat, you make a *Decision*, and then you *Act* (the reaction).

You quickly switch from Alert Mode to Crisis Mode by stepping laterally to the left or the right. At this point you should dodge his attack and then sprint away from the X. By moving off the X and out of the focus of the adrenalin-hyped bum, you have caused him to readjust his perception of you, and ideally to therefore decide to back off.

Bottom line. GET OFF THE X AS SOON AS POSSIBLE!

Okay, now let's talk worst-case scenario. Your Modes of Awareness cycle has failed you. You have been caught off guard and are standing smack center on the X. The bum was not actually just a bum looking for some cash, but an operative, and before you know it, you are taped up, blindfolded, and in the trunk of a car.

Let's rewind. What could you have done differently? If you're taken by surprise, fight, fight, fight! Remember, the attacker does not want a fight, and if you increase the time on the X by struggling, you will upend the attacker's speed and timeline.

Scream and yell like a banshee, minimizing the attacker's stealth and increasing Third-Party Awareness. You want people to see you being attacked. You want people to see your attackers, the car they are driving, and every other detail possible. Decrease the effectiveness of restraints by fighting as hard as you can and don't stop. Take every opportunity to claw, crawl, or run. If after all that, you still find yourself trapped in the trunk of a moving car...

Escape

There is a point of no return where you may have to stop fighting, keep your wits about you, and surrender temporarily. Some events that might force capitulation could be the barrel of a gun pressed against your head, being overpowered by several attackers, being tasered or stun-gunned, or receiving several substantial blows to the head. Point being, you want to live, not die. Accepting defeat temporarily will increase your survivability.

But it's not over yet. Even while you temporarily surrender, you should be transitioning between modes and using your OODA loop to survey the environment. Most people think there are only two options: rescue or death. Escape never crosses their minds. If you're prepared, you won't even think about rescue or death, because you will be too busy making your way back home.

Two tools to carry at all times: a razor blade and a handcuff key. You can hide these in a variety of locations, as long as it's someplace you can get to if your hands are behind your back and your feet are tied together. Most people can slide their wrists down their back to their feet, so you could tuck it in your waistline somewhere. Or you can keep it in the soles of your shoes. But wherever it is, it will require a bit of contortion to get to, so practice getting yourself out. That's what Houdini would do. The best time to free yourself is situation-dependent, but usually, the sooner the better. Too much time in custody could lead to detailed searches, being stripped naked, or death.

Your goal is to escape from your captors, but first you're going to have to escape from your restraints. The most popular restraint used by criminals and terrorists alike is tape, specifically clear-threaded packing tape. It's cheap, available worldwide, and faster to use than rope, chains, handcuffs, or zip ties.

If you're being restrained, the good news is that someone wants you around for a while. You are alive and being given a chance to turn the tables on your captors. Work fast and keep your wits about you.

Become a Houdini

Like most kids, I was mystified by magic. While traveling with my family in Hong Kong, I was lured by street vendors selling close-up, sleight-of-hand magic tricks. The vendors would perform a trick and wouldn't reveal how it was done until the purchase of the trick. Before I knew it, I had twenty-plus tricks. Thanks, Dad. Over time I became really good at close-up magic. Whether it was coins, spongy balls, playing cards, or handkerchiefs, I was hooked. And I was always asked, "How did you do that?" Of course, a magician never reveals his secrets.

There are some magic tricks worth revealing, however, because they have the power to save your life. Many come from the great magician, Harry Houdini, who figured out the process of escape decades ago.

One of Houdini's rules of escape certainly applies to escaping the wolf. It is this: *never attempt to perform an escape that you aren't certain you'll achieve.* This means that whether the restraint method is tape, rope, chain, or cuffs, you must practice to be proficient. It also means that if the possibility of death starts to raise its ugly head, you must stop the fight and act accordingly in order to survive.

For Houdini, of course, escapes weren't about life and death, but about showmanship. Audiences would flock to see his performances. The real attraction was his persona and his *presentation.*

The takeaway for those of us engaged in an escape that *is* a matter of life and death is *presentation.* We're not talking about showmanship, but instead about how you present yourself to the wolf when he is taking you captive. Your presentation is your setup for a successful escape. In his 1921 book, *Magical Rope Ties and Escapes*, Houdini explained many of his strategies:

> If the committee...begin to make more knots than suits you, it will be well to swell the muscles, expand the chest, slightly hunch the shoulders, and hold the arm a little away from the sides. After a little practice you will find that such artifices will enable you to balk the most knowing ones. You should always wear a coat when submitting to this tie, as that will be found to be an added help in obtaining slack...

By creating gaps and doing what I call "getting big" during capture, you create slack in the tape, rope, or chains used to subdue you. This is the art of presentation. You want to make your chest as big as possible, keep your elbows away from your sides, and keep your wrists, knees, and ankles apart. Remember, while on the X, the attackers want to move fast and limit their exposure to public attention. You've already worn them out with a fight and made lots of noise. The attackers will be tired and working fast, and they likely won't be paying attention to how you are creating slack in their restraints. These first moments of capture are your best opportunity to set yourself up for a sooner-rather-than-later escape.

Houdini wasn't opposed to a little trickery, and you shouldn't be either.

A sharp knife with a hook-shaped blade should be concealed somewhere on the person, as it may be found useful in case some of the first, carefully tied knots prove troublesome. A short piece cut from the end of the rope will never be missed.

Houdini's amazing ability to escape from handcuffs led to his discovery by vaudeville impresario Martin Beck in 1899. Although Houdini was hardly the first or only performer to do handcuff escapes, he would take the act to a new level over the next several years. As the "Handcuff King," Houdini gained his first measure of fame. There was no one "secret" to Houdini's ability to escape from handcuffs, but rather a combination of technical knowledge, physical skill, and trickery. Most of the time Houdini used a key hidden in or smuggled into the cabinet or jail cell, either pre-staged within his clothing or smuggled in by an assistant. Depending on how he was bound, Houdini would manipulate the keys with his hands—sometimes using specially designed extension rods—or with his teeth.

Houdini also knew tricks for opening many of the simpler types of cuffs without keys. In *Handcuff Secrets*, a book he published in 1910 to discourage the legion of imitators trying to ride his coattails, Houdini wrote,

> You can open the majority of the old-time cuffs with a shoestring. By simply making a loop in the string, you can lasso the end of the screw in the lock and yank the

bolt back, and so open the cuff in as clean a manner as if opened with the original key.

And as he demonstrated in his own defense during a German slander trial in 1902, some cuffs could be opened simply by being banged against a hard surface, which might include a lead plate fastened at the knee under his trousers.

Houdini also used tricks that didn't involve opening locks. If presented with a particularly difficult lock, he might insist it be placed higher on his forearm, and then simply slip these loose cuffs over his wrists.

THE TAKEAWAY

Travelcraft skills are like playing chess. The move you make now sets you up for success later. Fortunately, the bad guys typically play checkers and don't notice what your moves could tell them about the future.

So avoid alleyways. In restaurants, sit facing the door. Pay for your meals first. Know that pepper and salt burn the eyes, and always know where the back door is located.

"Travel is more than the seeing of sights; it is a change that goes on, deep and permanent, in the ideas of living."

—MIRIAM BEARD

PRACTICE ASSIGNMENT– THIRD-PARTY AWARENESS

IT'S TEMPTING, BUT DON'T MESS WITH SURVEILLANCE

THIS CHAPTER HAS SHOWN YOU HOW TO DETERMINE IF YOU ARE BEING targeted for surveillance. You've learned how to identify when your hotel room or car might have been tampered with and how to determine if technical surveillance equipment has been installed. Those are sobering possibilities, but they are possibilities you should take seriously. They may never happen to you, but it's always better to be prepared. Let's take a look at a real-life example—an example of what you *shouldn't* do when under surveillance.

PRACTICAL EXAMPLE

- Semi-permissive environment (area with some government control)

- Being followed by a surveillance team

When a host nation has limited surveillance resources, a lack of training, or just the desire to intimidate you and prevent you from getting work done, they may perform what is known as a "bumper lock." This tactic consists of obvious overt surveillance of you and your activities. In short, the surveillance team is always right behind you, in your rear-view mirror, opening the supermarket door for you, there when you wake up, and tucking you in at night. It is stressful and intimidating, and decision-making while under this kind of coverage is difficult.

Who is doing this? Is it a government-sponsored surveillance team who think you are a spy? Is it a bunch of criminals who want to steal your rental car? Or are they a bunch of terrorists who want to chop your head off? You cannot positively determine who "they" are or what their intentions are, so what do you do? This is probably one of the most difficult equations, and the answer resides within the person being followed. A true spy would tell you to embrace surveillance, bore them, and get them to fall in love with you so that you can take advantage of them when it's time.

I experienced this situation when I landed in a former Eastern bloc country to survey possible threat vulnerabilities to a US installation. I was immediately bumper locked from the airport to the hotel. In my rearview mirror, I could see a white Toyota Corolla with four large white males crammed inside. The chances were very high that they were government-sponsored surveillance curious to see what I was doing and why I was there. I figured that because of lack of resources and training, it was easier for them to just bumper lock and see what I would do, how I would react, and what my level of training was rather than to engage in covert surveillance. My job was to embrace them, act like I did not see them, and carry on with my job in a very boring, unappealing manner.

Fine. But eventually I got bored with this particular assignment and decided to have fun with my new friends. Again, boredom is a serious detriment to good work. So, one day as I drove around town, doing nothing but shopping, eating, and playing tourist, I decided to play with the team of goons. As you may or may not know, other less-fortunate government agencies think that the United States has thousands of invisible Unmanned Airborne Vehicles (UAVs) soaring through the skies like eagles. They think these gunships are hovering on standby in every country ready to launch rockets at anything that moves, and that each American spy has a satellite issued to him or her like a pair of jungle boots. Obviously not true, but why not take advantage of this myth, just for fun?

At each of my stops, I would park, exit my rental car, look at my watch, and then look at the sky. The goons didn't notice at first. They would typically park and exit their Toyota. One would follow me into whatever establishment, and the others would hang out and smoke. By the second day and third stop, they must have noticed my strange habit of looking at my watch and then looking up at the sky. At the fourth stop, all goons stayed in their vehicle and rolled down the windows. Four heads popped out, peering up to the sky trying to see what I was looking at. I couldn't help but laugh (to myself of course).

At the end of the day, I returned to my hotel room, where I found all the contents of my luggage scattered neatly about my room, the furniture rearranged, and my toilet filled with a fresh present. Touché!

STUDY GUIDE QUESTIONS

Should I have taunted the bad guys who had me under surveillance?

What would you have done in that situation?

STUDY GUIDE ANSWERS

Should I have taunted the bad guys who had me under surveillance?

As tempting as it was, it's never wise to taunt surveillance, nor is it smart to reveal your skills or training. This gives a surveillance team a reason to tighten up on you. Also, never assume that the surveillance is government-sponsored. You could be dealing with terrorists.

Keep in mind, a trained spy can usually use his training, experience, and other resources to determine the nature of surveillance. A businessperson lacks those skills. You could be followed by government agents who think you are a spy dressed like a businessperson, or that you have trade secrets that would benefit their economy. Remember, governments all over the world are committing time and resources to corporate espionage, hoping to obtain the latest information that could help their economy. But it could simply be bad guys wanting to take your Rolex.

Whatever the nature of the threat, it's imperative that you use your Modes of Awareness cycle to detect it, and then behave responsibly. Always report surveillance to your corporate chief security officer (if you are a businessperson), the embassy, and the individual or entity you are doing business with, in that order. Your report to your company will be logged for that destination. The report to the embassy will be investigated through host nation contacts. Your report to whomever you're doing business with will let them know that you are smarter than the average bear. The more who know, the better, particularly if you should happen to suddenly disappear.

What would you have done in this situation?

When you think you're being followed, keep these things in mind:

- Never take surveillance lightly.

- Always remain calm.

- Always use your Modes of Awareness cycle. Don't get rearview mirror tunnel vision—you can be surveilled from the front just as easily as from behind.

- Always keep surveillance happy.

- Exhibit good Personal Awareness. Always appear boring, unimportant, and unappealing. They may decide to stop watching you and shift to someone else.

- Practice good Situational Awareness. Always take note of the license plate number, vehicle make, model, and color of the surveillance vehicle that is tracking you. If possible, use the A-H diagram (from Chapter 2) to remember the human characteristics for each surveillance team member.

NOTES:

_____

_____

_____

_____

_____

_____

_____

_____

_____

_____

_____

_____

_____

_____

_____

_____

_____

_____

_____

6

THREATS

THE WOLF'S MANY FORMS

"The traveler was active; he went strenuously in search of people, of adventure, of experience. The tourist is passive; he expects interesting things to happen to him. He goes 'sight-seeing.'"

—DANIEL J. BOORSTIN

A KEY ELEMENT IN AVOIDING OR ESCAPING THE WOLF IS UNDERSTAND-ing what the wolf looks like, researching where he operates, and determining the odds of running into him. Threats (or wolves) appear in many shapes and forms. In this chapter, I will discuss threats with a broad brush, identifying some of the more common threats and showing you how to deal with them. But because new threats are constantly emerging and every location has particularities of its own, the information in this chapter should be used only as a jumping-off point for your own, destination-specific research.

Threats are usually unknown adversaries, obstacles, or situations that take you by surprise. That sounds simple, and it is, but that simplicity means that they can be avoided or countered with proper preparation. They can't catch you by surprise if you're ready. Of course, some threats are unavoidable and will take you by surprise no matter how prepared you are, but by practicing good Personal Awareness and Situational Awareness, you can reduce those surprises dramatically.

For this discussion, THREAT is not only our topic, but also an acronym categorizing risks of a variety of natures—**T**echnological, **H**ealth, **R**aids, **E**nvironment, **A**gencies, and **T**errorism. The following broad definitions lay out common worldwide dangers in each of these categories.

Technological Threats. Technological threats include audio collection devices, video collection devices, tracking devices, cell phone exploitation, and laptop exploitation.

Health Threats. Health threats include viruses, bacteria, chemicals, and other harmful substances spread human-to-human, airborne-to-human, water- or food-to-human, and vector-to-human. I will cover some of the more popular disease processes, signs and symptoms, and treatment, but your research should also identify poisonous reptiles, insects, and any other animals that could pose a threat in specific locations.

Raids/Robbery. These types of threats include organized assaults conducted by criminals or terrorists. By definition, a criminal is a person guilty of a crime or crimes. Criminals commit theft, rape, murder, and everything in between. The most significant raids are kidnapping, carjacking, and hostage situations.

Environmental Threats. Environmental threats include natural events like hurricanes, tsunamis, winter storms, volcano eruptions, and mudslides. I will discuss some of these disasters and actions to be taken, but you will need to look up specifics related to the area you plan to visit.

Agency Threats. Certain intelligence and law enforcement agencies are devoted to collecting information related to host government security and defense. I will identify and discuss several different agencies, their intentions, and how they might affect you, though as always you should do your own research before going anywhere.

Terrorism. A terrorist is a person or group using unlawful acts of violence to influence, coerce, or strike fear into people for ideological, political, or religious gains. Currently, there is not an internationally agreed-upon definition of terrorism. We will look at terrorist facts, groups, and tactics, but look into potential terrorist threats and specifics about active groups related to the area you plan to visit.

I've said this a lot, but I have to say it again—*research is essential.* Perhaps you've heard of the "Seven Ps"—"Proper Prior Planning Prevents Piss Poor Performance"? There's a reason this saying has such resonance.

Take the time to determine possible threats before you embark. Start by writing THREAT vertically on a sheet of paper. Look up your country online and use what you learn to begin filling in the blanks. Open source information is readily available online.

TECHNOLOGICAL THREATS

It was only about sixty years ago that the first computer was developed. It filled an entire room. Today, technology is micro in size and giant in capability, with a price tag even the poorest wolf can afford. Even in the farthest corners of the earth, you'll find internet cafes filled with people surfing the web, emailing, and socializing. But what are they really up to?

Methods of Collection

The world's most common methods of information collection all involve photo, video, audio, and tracking devices. Manned or unmanned, the technologies can be used right out of the box and concealed in just about anything.

Photo and Video

Cameras are everywhere these days. I've read that the average American is recorded by security cameras an average of 230 times a day, and that number is growing. It doesn't take a rocket scientist to understand how that is possible, given all the cameras we encounter over the course of a given day via mobile device or at traffic stops, ATM machines, stores, restaurants, gas stations, and more. In other countries, like England, that number is much higher. British intelligence can literally track a person who stays in London from the time of arrival at the airport to the time of departure at the airport. All cameras are synced together and "hand off" targeted individuals from camera to camera intuitively. There are more than 5.2 million CCTV cameras in England. Are you paranoid yet?

Who Would Take Your Picture?

Individuals and entities who might be taking your photo when you are traveling include host nation law enforcement officials, intelligence agencies, members of the military, public transportation agencies, private security forces, shopping mall security, and traffic-related systems. That is certainly intimidating. But here is a dose of reality: none of these agencies employ enough people to observe every camera feed in real time. Though most of these systems are on all the time and recording, they are reviewed only in the event of a crisis.

Who Uses Concealed Cameras?

Any of the above entities could use concealed cameras. Shopping districts use concealed cameras to watch the cash register, stored inventory, entrances, and exits. And host nation intelligence agents, terrorists, and criminals alike will take an interest in you if you match a certain profile or if your demeanor says, "Look at me, I am a bad news American." Whatever you do, don't search your hotel room and rental cars for hidden cameras. If "they" are watching, then you just compromised yourself by visibly searching for signs of surveillance. Assume your hotel and rental car have either passive or active concealed cameras and act accordingly.

Countering Image Capture

The first step in countering image capture is to assume that your picture is being taken at every minute of the day and night—so you want to make sure they are photographing what *you* want them to. Through proper Total Awareness techniques, specifically projection and demeanor, you will give observers nothing to note. When in Alert Mode, you will observe the cameras, orientate yourself accordingly, decide upon alternate routes, and take action to avoid future cameras. But the reality is that for every camera you spot, there are dozens that you don't.

A proper demeanor will reveal nothing to the people on the opposite side of those cameras. Depending on your occupation and reason for being in that country, you may decide to use a light disguise, take advantage of lighting, or stress the limitations of the cameras you encounter. A light disguise consists of umbrellas, hats, sunglasses, and other accessories that could make identification difficult. Please keep in mind: if the attire isn't common within a particular culture, wearing it may bring more attention to you, rather than less. Americans are the only ones who wear sunglasses religiously. Very few people overseas wear baseball-style caps except Americans. If you wear both, consider yourself targeted.

With or without accessories, you can use the sun or other light sources to your advantage. Putting yourself between the camera and a light source will effectively backlight you and make any image useless. Stressing the limitations of the camera's field of view and focal length can work to your advantage. For example, cash machine (ATM) cameras are angled and set to focus on face-size objects eight to twelve inches away. Passing these machines within a distance greater than twelve inches will effectively result in a blurry image of you or your vehicle.

Audio Devices

In addition to watching you, any of the above entities may want to hear what you have to say. Depending on why you are in the country, intelligence agencies, law enforcement, terrorists, and criminals may want information from you. Information is what creates action, whether against you or others. How is audio information collected? The most popular listening devices are ears. You never know who is listening, and if you have the gift of gab, assume someone will hear you. Your cab driver is absolutely able to listen to your phone call. Remember Third-Party Awareness and Communication Security from Chapter 5? This would be a good time to review it. Ultimately, good Personal Awareness will prevent this kind of collection—or at the very least prevent anyone from hearing anything you don't want them to.

The next most prevalent audio collection device is the mobile phone. There are programs that can be downloaded to a cell phone that allow a user to turn on another person's cell phone microphone without its owner knowing it. This allows them to use the targeted phone as a real-time listening device. These programs were developed for parents wanting to listen to their teenagers, but there's no age limit on the programs, and they can be used against you. Some host nation governments have systems that listen to all cell phone conversations originating in their country. Mobile phones are the single biggest communication platform—and therefore also the single biggest technical surveillance threat.

Your Phone: What to Do?

The reality is that most of us need to have our phones with us at all times. They tell us when our next appointment is and where to go, and they allow us to be in communication with just about everyone in our lives, anytime.

Phones are great. They're also a crutch, and something that can easily be used against you. If you've got your head down, looking at your phone, you are *not* engaged in Situational Awareness. If you've turned on a maps app and you're using that to navigate your way around an unfamiliar city, you are *not* engaged in Personal Awareness. *You are making yourself a target.*

So what's the solution? I'm tempted to tell you to be like me and never use a mobile phone to begin with—or, if you absolutely need one, to purchase a burner phone and sim card once you're in a different country. But the reality is that you probably need all the information and access your phone provides you, and it's just not practical to do without it.

I could tell you to keep your phone off, but unfortunately a phone that appears to be off can still be used as a listening device. You can't remove the battery and ensure it's genuinely off because the battery has its own processor. I could tell you to keep it in a faraday pouch, designed to cut off service, but even those aren't 100 percent effective, because cell signals are so strong these days it takes an extraordinary amount of metal fabric to actually block all those signals a phone receives and emits. Think about it—Bluetooth, CDMA, GSM, satellite, Wi-Fi...the list goes on and on. We're paying so much money for our phones these days that they better get a signal *anywhere*...and so they do, even inside a faraday pouch.

Here's the thing—that's also good news. Yes, it means you can be tracked...but sometimes, you *want* to be. If the worst happens and you get kidnapped, your phone will track your location, wherever you are taken. Keep it on silent and hidden, and the authorities will be able to find you.

And the rest of the time? Just keep your head up. Check your phone and know where you're headed before you leave your hotel room, so that you can keep your eyes up. Have your route planned before you start walking or driving anywhere. Keep your phone on you so that you always know where it is, and use a good password, okay? Just in case.

Concealed Audio Devices

Concealable audio devices can be employed just about anywhere, and if installed correctly, will be undetectable. These "bugs" come in all shapes and sizes. They can be installed in your hotel room, rental cars, popular bars, office, home, and even an embassy. Don't actively look for devices. If there is video, you just burned yourself. Don't think turning the TV on is going to help, either. Readily available software can cancel out background noise. The best measure of protection is to always assume someone is listening, especially in your hotel rooms and rental cars. Demeanor, demeanor, demeanor!

Tracking

Tracking via technical device can be accomplished in several ways. Let's start with your passport, which probably contains a radio frequency identification (RFID) card—every passport issued after October 2006 is outfitted with this little computer chip. These chips have 64 kilobytes of memory, which contain your date of birth, nationality, gender, place of birth, and digital photograph. Basically, everything that's printed in your passport is also on the chip. This measure is meant to improve security, but basically it means that all your info can be scanned covertly, including by criminals or terrorists. And not only that—this chip allows you to be tracked. If enough electrons are pumped into the RFID remotely, the passport becomes a beacon. With the right receiver and software, your location can be identified. Now, it would take a very technologically advanced intelligence or law enforcement agency, but the threat is there.

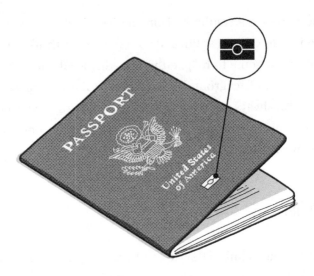

Remember, your mobile phone can be a tracking device as well. The government of any country owns the cell phone towers with which your mobile phone communicates regularly. It doesn't take much to watch your movements.

Rental cars are typically tracked for inventory control, vehicle relocation (if stolen or abandoned), and emergencies. Most use a cell phone–based technology. Once again, assume you are being tracked regardless of environment.

Concealed Tracking Devices

These days, anyone can purchase tracking devices right off the internet. Extremely user-friendly and cheap, they come in a variety of shapes and sizes. Some are the size of credit cards, while others look like a large thumb drive or a black brick. Depending on the device, they can be tracked in real time by websites, special receivers, and even mobile phones. Other devices have to be physically removed to view stored data on a computer. They can be installed deep into a compartment in a vehicle or slapped under the bumper.

Laptop Security

Thinking of taking your laptop on the road? It's a great way to work and stay in touch when traveling. Believe you're all set because you have a firewall, up-to-date antivirus software, a strong password, and encrypted data? Not quite. Once again, it's about awareness and taking a few simple precautionary steps. Consider doing the following to keep your laptop safe—and in your possession—when you're on the road:

- Treat it like the mountain of cash (or information) it is.

- Get it out of the car. Don't leave it behind—ever.

- Try not to leave your laptop anywhere, including in your hotel room. If you must leave the laptop, use a security cable to attach it to something immovable or really heavy and hard to move.

- If you're in an office or restaurant, keep it off the floor, or at least between your feet.

- Keep passwords separate—not near your laptop or case.

- Don't leave it "for just a sec," no matter where you are. Don't trust anyone, even those nice people in the coffee shop.

- Pay attention in airports, especially at security checkpoints.

- Turn on the "Find My Device" features in all your devices.

- Report a missing laptop IMMEDIATELY. If it's stolen, report the theft to the local authorities. Report a business laptop disappearance immediately to your employer. If it's your personal laptop and you fear identity theft, visit the Federal Trade Commission's identity theft web page for instructions.

Data Protection

There are a lot of different encryption software options out there, and at this point they're all pretty good at what they do.

The best advice I can offer is to double-wrap anything you're sending. That means compressing your documents into a zip file, and make that file password-protected. Then, before you send it, wrap it up again in a PGP (Pretty Good Privacy) encryption, just to be extra cautious.

That way, the person on the receiving end needs to have *both* passwords in order to open the document (it goes without saying that the passwords should not be identical).

Web Browsing

I'd love to tell you that Firefox is the most secure web browser, or Chrome, or Snowden-endorsed Tor, but the reality is that they're all competing, so it's always shifting. I would pay attention to who owns what. Chrome is owned by Google, so surprise surprise, it's tracking everything you do in order to better advertise to you. Firefox is open source, which helps you make sure nothing too nefarious is going on, but it's also pretty buggy, and navigating its support system makes it a pain to use. Tor is slow like dial-up.

Personally, I don't care that Chrome or Facebook or Alexa is tracking my every move. I'm not doing anything I need to keep hidden from anyone, not these days. If they make it easier for me to buy something I want, great! That's one chore that they just made a little less onerous. If you're not doing anything wrong, who cares?

But that's for advertising purposes. If it turns out your preferred browser or email carrier is suddenly owned by China or Russia, then all that tracking is likely to result in stolen intellectual property, not in a thoughtful gift for Mother's Day.

To conclude, a very wise man, KB, once told me:

- Someone can always see you; don't give them a reason to watch.

- Someone can always hear you; don't give them a reason to listen.

- Someone can always find you; don't give them a reason to look.

HEALTH THREATS

Health threats are global and inescapable to a certain degree. You can wash your hands, burn your food, spray everything down with bleach, and still get sick. There are millions of diseases that hide throughout the globe, some more common than others. I am going to cover diseases that I have either personally obtained overseas or witnessed someone else get, as well as other diseases you may encounter more frequently. As always, I cannot overemphasize the importance of country studies prior to departure. With a country study, you can determine what diseases you are likely to encounter, in what seasons these diseases are more prevalent, what immunizations are required, and whether there is any available prophylaxis that can be taken to combat them.

You can also research other types of threats that may jeopardize your health. For example, the World Health Organization (WHO) has launched a website containing a database of approved antivenoms to treat the 2.5 million people who suffer from venomous snake bites each year—with an estimated 100,000 of them resulting in death. Out of more than 3,000 species of snakes in the world, some 600 are venomous. In addition to poisonous snakebites, there are poisonous spider and insect bites. It's important to research all the various health hazards you might encounter in the areas you plan to visit.

Malaria

Key Facts

- There were 230 million cases of malaria in 2019, causing about 410,000 deaths, mostly among African children.

- Malaria is preventable and curable.

- Approximately half of the world's population is at risk of malaria, particularly those living in lower-income countries.

- Travelers from malaria-free areas to disease "hot spots" are especially vulnerable to the disease.

Malaria is caused by parasites of the species *Plasmodium*. The parasites are spread to people when the people are bitten by infected mosquitoes.

Transmission

Malaria transmission rates can differ depending on local factors, such as rainfall patterns (mosquitoes breed in wet conditions), the proximity of mosquito breeding sites to people, and types of mosquito species in the area. Some regions have a fairly constant number of cases throughout the year. These countries are termed "malaria endemic." In other areas, there are "malaria seasons," usually coinciding with the rainy season.

Large and devastating epidemics can occur when the mosquito-borne parasite is introduced into areas where people have had little prior contact with the infecting parasite and have little or no immunity to malaria, or when people with low immunity move into areas where malaria cases are constant.

These epidemics can be triggered by wet weather conditions and further aggravated by floods or mass population movements driven by conflict.

Symptoms

The common first symptoms—fever, headache, chills, and vomiting—usually appear ten to fifteen days after a person is infected. If not treated promptly with effective medicines, malaria can cause severe illness and is often fatal.

At-Risk Populations

Most cases and deaths are in sub-Saharan Africa. Asia, Latin America, the Middle East, and parts of Europe, however, are also affected.

- Travelers from malaria-free regions, with little or no immunity, who go to areas with high disease rates are very vulnerable.

- Nonimmune pregnant women are at high risk of malaria. The illness can result in high rates of miscarriage and cause more than 10 percent of maternal deaths (soaring to a 50 percent death rate in cases of severe disease) annually.

- Semi-immune pregnant women risk severe anemia and impaired fetal growth even if they show no signs of acute disease. An estimated 200,000 of their infants die annually as a result of malaria infection during pregnancy.

- HIV-infected pregnant women are also at increased risk.

Treatments

- Early treatment of malaria shortens its duration, prevents complications, and lessens the likelihood of death. Because of its considerable drag on health in low-income countries, malaria disease management is an essential part of global development. Treatment aims to cure patients of the disease rather than diminish the number of parasites carried by an infected person.

- The best available treatment, particularly for *P. falciparum* malaria, is a combination of drugs known as artemisinin-based combination therapies (ACTs). The growing potential for parasite resistance to these medicines, however, is undermining malaria control efforts. There are no effective alternatives to artemisinins for the treatment of malaria either on the market or nearing the end of the drug-development process.

Prevention

• For travelers, malaria can be prevented through chemoprophylaxis, which suppresses the blood stage of malaria infections, thereby preventing malaria disease. For pregnant women living in moderate-to-high transmission areas, WHO recommends at least three doses of intermittent preventive treatment with sulfadoxine-pyrimethamine at each scheduled antenatal visit after the first trimester. Similarly, for infants living in high-transmission areas of Africa, three doses of intermittent preventive treatment with sulfadoxine-pyrimethamine are recommended, delivered alongside routine vaccinations.

Anthrax

Anthrax is a serious disease caused by *Bacillus anthracis*, a bacterium that forms spores. (A bacterium spore is a cell that is dormant (asleep) but may come to life with the right conditions.)

There are three types of anthrax:

- Skin (cutaneous)

- Lungs (inhalation)

- Digestive (gastrointestinal)

Transmission

- Anthrax is not known to spread from one person to another.

- Anthrax from animals: Humans can become infected with anthrax by handling products derived from infected animals or by breathing in anthrax spores from infected animal products (like wool, for example). People also can become infected with gastrointestinal anthrax by eating undercooked meat from infected animals.

- Anthrax also can be used as a weapon. In the United States in 2001, anthrax was deliberately spread through the postal system by sending letters with powder containing anthrax. This act caused twenty-two cases of anthrax infection.

How Dangerous Is Anthrax?

The Centers for Disease Control and Prevention classifies agents with recognized bioterrorism potential into three priority areas (A, B, and C). Anthrax is classified as a Category A agent. Category A agents are those that:

- Pose the greatest possible threat for a detrimental effect on public health

- May spread across a large area or require public awareness

- Must be met with a great deal of planning in order to protect the public's health

In most cases, early treatment with antibiotics can cure cutaneous anthrax. Even if untreated, 80 percent of people who become infected with cutaneous anthrax do not die. Gastrointestinal anthrax is more serious because between one-fourth to more than one-half of the cases lead to death. Inhalation anthrax is much more severe. In 2001, about half of the cases of inhalation anthrax ended in death.

Symptoms

The symptoms (warning signs) of anthrax are different, depending on the type of the disease:

- **Cutaneous**. The first symptom is a small sore that develops into a blister. The blister then develops into a skin ulcer with a black area in the center. The sore, blister, and ulcer do not hurt.

- **Gastrointestinal**. The first symptoms are nausea, loss of appetite, bloody diarrhea, and fever, followed by bad stomach pain.

- **Inhalation**. The first symptoms of inhalation anthrax are cold or flu-like symptoms and can include a sore throat, mild fever, and muscle aches. Later symptoms include cough, chest discomfort, shortness of breath, tiredness, and muscle aches. (Caution: do not assume that just because a person has cold or flu symptoms they have inhalation anthrax.)

How Soon Do Infected People Get Sick?

Symptoms can appear within seven days of coming in contact with the bacterium for all three types of anthrax. For inhalation anthrax, symptoms can appear within a week, but may take up to forty-two days to appear.

Treatment

Antibiotics are used to treat all three types of anthrax. Early identification and treatment are important, as is preventive treatment in the face of suspected exposure.

- **Prevention after exposure.** If a person is exposed to anthrax but is not yet sick, healthcare providers will use antibiotics (such as ciprofloxacin, levofloxacin, doxycycline, or penicillin) combined with the anthrax vaccine to prevent anthrax infection.

- **Treatment after infection**. Treatment is usually a sixty-day course of antibiotics. Success depends on the type of anthrax and how soon treatment begins.

Prevention

There is a vaccine to prevent anthrax, but it is not typically available to the general public. However, anyone who may be exposed to anthrax, including certain members of the US armed forces, laboratory workers, and workers who may enter or re-enter contaminated areas, may get the vaccine. In the event of an attack that used anthrax as a weapon, people who were exposed would receive the vaccine.

Botulism

Botulism is a muscle-paralyzing disease caused by a toxin made by a bacterium called *Clostridium botulinum.*

Key Facts

There are three main types of botulism:

- Food-borne botulism occurs when a person ingests pre-formed toxins, leading to illness within a few hours to days. Food-borne botulism is considered a public health emergency because the contaminated food may still be available to other persons besides the patient.

- Infant botulism occurs in a small number of susceptible infants each year who harbor *C. botulinum* in their intestinal tract.

- Wound botulism occurs when wounds are infected with *C. botulinum*, which secretes the toxin.

Symptoms

With food-borne botulism, symptoms begin within six hours to two weeks (most commonly between twelve and thirty-six hours) after eating food that contains the toxin. Symptoms of botulism include double vision, blurred vision, drooping eyelids, slurred speech, difficulty swallowing, dry mouth, and muscle weakness that moves down the body, always affecting the shoulders first, then the upper arms, lower arms, thighs, calves, etc. Paralysis of breathing muscles can cause a person to stop breathing and die unless assistance with breathing (mechanical ventilation) is provided.

Transmission

Botulism is not spread from one person to another. Food-borne botulism can occur in all age groups.

Treatment and Prevention

A supply of antitoxin against botulism is maintained by the CDC. The antitoxin is effective in reducing the severity of symptoms if administered early in the course of the disease. Most patients eventually recover after weeks to months of supportive care. In March 2021, there was a food-borne botulism outbreak in Denmark following a private party. Three adults were hospitalized, and all were treated with an antitoxin, with their stool samples studied to identify the likely culprit. The thing is, depending on where you are, there may be a shortage of antitoxin, so you must be aware that it may not always be readily available.

COVID-19

COVID-19 is the disease caused by a coronavirus called SARS-CoV-2.

Symptoms

The most common symptoms of COVID-19 are:

- Fever

- Dry cough

- Fatigue

Other symptoms that are less common and may affect some patients include:

- Loss of taste or smell

- Nasal congestion

- Conjunctivitis (also known as red eyes)

- Sore throat

- Headache

- Muscle or joint pain

- Different types of skin rash

- Nausea or vomiting

- Diarrhea

- Chills or dizziness

Symptoms of severe COVID-19 disease include:

- Shortness of breath

- Loss of appetite

- Confusion

- Persistent pain or pressure in the chest

- High temperature (above 100.4° F)

Transmission

The virus can spread from an infected person's mouth or nose in small liquid particles when they cough, sneeze, speak, sing, or breathe. These particles range from larger respiratory droplets to smaller aerosols.

- Current evidence suggests that the virus spreads mainly between people who are in close contact with each other, typically within three feet (short range). A person can be infected when aerosols or droplets containing the virus are inhaled or come directly into contact with the eyes, nose, or mouth.

- The virus can also spread in poorly ventilated and/ or crowded indoor settings, where people tend to spend longer periods of time. This is because aerosols remain suspended in the air or travel farther than three feet (long range).

Treatment and Prevention

There are several vaccinations available, and though none of them are 100 percent effective, they do significantly decrease the risk of infection and also decrease the severity of the illness, should a breakthrough infection occur.

Salmonellosis

Salmonellosis is an infection with bacteria called Salmonella. Most persons infected with Salmonella develop diarrhea, fever, and abdominal cramps twelve to seventy-two hours after infection. The illness usually lasts four to seven days, and most persons recover without treatment. However, in some persons, the diarrhea may be so severe that the patient needs to be hospitalized. In these patients, the Salmonella infection may spread from the intestines to the bloodstream, and then to other body sites, at which point it can cause death unless the person is treated promptly with antibiotics. The elderly, infants, and those with impaired immune systems are more likely to have a severe illness.

Symptoms

Many different kinds of illnesses can cause diarrhea, fever, or abdominal cramps. In order to positively identify Salmonella as the cause of the illness, laboratory tests must detect Salmonella in the stools of an infected person. These tests are sometimes not performed unless the laboratory is specifically instructed to look for the organism. Once Salmonella has been identified, further testing can determine its specific type and which antibiotics could be used to treat it.

Treatment

Most Salmonella infections resolve in five to seven days and do not require treatment. Persons with severe diarrhea may require rehydration, often with intravenous fluids. Antibiotics are not usually necessary unless the infection spreads from the intestines, in which case it can be treated with ampicillin, gentamicin, trimethoprim/sulfamethoxazole, or ciprofloxacin. Unfortunately, some Salmonella bacteria have become resistant to antibiotics, largely as a result of the use of antibiotics to promote growth of feed animals.

Long-Term Implications

Persons with diarrhea usually recover completely, although it may be several months before their bowel habits are entirely normal. A small number of persons who are infected with Salmonella will go on to develop pains in their joints, irritation of the eyes, and painful urination. This is called Reiter's syndrome. It can last for months or years and can lead to chronic arthritis, which is difficult to treat. Antibiotic treatment does not make a difference in whether or not the person later develops arthritis.

Transmission

Salmonella live in the intestinal tracts of humans and other animals, including birds, and are usually transmitted to humans via foods contaminated with animal feces. Contaminated foods usually look and smell normal, and are often of animal origin—beef, poultry, milk, or eggs are common examples—but all foods, including vegetables, may become contaminated. Raw foods of animal origin are frequently contaminated, but fortunately, thorough cooking kills Salmonella. Food may also become contaminated by an infected food handler who forgot to wash his or her hands with soap after using the bathroom.

Salmonella may also be found in the feces of some pets, especially those with diarrhea. Individuals can become infected if they do not wash their hands after contact with these feces. Reptiles are particularly likely to harbor Salmonella, and people should always wash their hands immediately after handling a reptile, even if the reptile is healthy. Adults should also make sure children wash their hands after handling a reptile.

Prevention

There is no vaccine to prevent salmonellosis. Since foods of animal origin may be contaminated with Salmonella, try not to eat raw or undercooked eggs, poultry, or meat. Be careful as you may not recognize that raw eggs are in some foods, such as homemade hollandaise sauce, homemade salad dressings, tiramisu, homemade ice cream, homemade mayonnaise, certain cocktails, cookie dough, and frostings. Poultry and meat, including hamburgers, should be well-cooked, not pink in the middle. Try not to consume raw or unpasteurized milk or other dairy products. Thoroughly wash produce before consuming.

Avoid cross-contamination of foods. Keep uncooked meats separate from produce, cooked foods, and ready-to-eat foods. Thoroughly wash hands, cutting boards, counters, knives, and other utensils after handling uncooked foods. Wash hands before handling any food, and between handling different food items. Individuals who have salmonellosis should not prepare food or pour water for others until they have been shown to no longer be carrying the Salmonella bacterium. Wash hands after contact with animal feces.

Cholera

Cholera is an acute diarrheal illness caused by infection of the intestine with the bacterium *Vibrio cholerae*. The infection is often mild or without symptoms, but can sometimes be severe. Approximately one in twenty infected persons has severe disease characterized by profuse watery diarrhea, vomiting, and leg cramps. In these persons, rapid loss of body fluids leads to dehydration and shock. Without treatment, death can occur within hours.

The risk for cholera is very low for US travelers visiting areas with epidemic cholera. If simple precautions are observed, contracting the disease is unlikely.

All travelers to areas where cholera has occurred should observe the following recommendations:

Drink only water that you have boiled or treated with chlorine or iodine. Other safe beverages include tea and coffee made with boiled water and carbonated bottled beverages with no ice. Eat only foods that have been thoroughly cooked and are still hot, or fruit that you have peeled yourself. Avoid undercooked or raw fish or shellfish, including ceviche. Make sure all vegetables are cooked. Avoid salads. Avoid foods and beverages from street vendors. Do not bring perishable seafood back to the United States.

A simple rule of thumb is: "Boil it, cook it, peel it, or forget it."

Boil it   **Cook it**   **Peel it**

OR FORGET IT!

BEYOND DISEASES

Air pollution has become a major health concern in many countries and regions of the world. Large cities, such as Beijing, Delhi, Mexico City, and Cairo, receive all the headlines, but many other less-populated areas suffer from poor air quality due to geography, weather patterns, volcanic activity, and the high-polluting industries found there. Symptoms to recognize if affected by air pollution include coughing; shortness of breath; wheezing; itchy, watery eyes; chest pain; nausea; and headaches.

Everyone is affected differently by air quality so, as with everything else, do your research and understand what you will be encountering during your travels. A couple of valuable resources on worldwide air pollution are the World Health Organization and AirNow.gov.

RAIDS/ROBBERY THREATS

An increasingly unstable economic situation worldwide means that crime will only increase. In all cases, your actions should be dictated by the reason you are in the country and the perceived risk. Choose your battles wisely in order to reduce unnecessary attention to yourself. If you are pick-pocketed, ask yourself whether it's really worth chasing the criminal down.

Crimes of interest, as they relate to the traveling professional, consist of some form of carjacking, kidnapping, or hostage and ransom operations. There are plenty more examples, but these are the crimes with potential for death. A large number of these crimes will be committed when you are approaching your vehicle or while driving, so the following section will cover the anatomy of and best responses to carjacking, kidnapping, and hostage-ransom crimes.

Carjacking

Carjacking has become one of the most prevalent crimes in many parts of the world, overtaking car theft as sophisticated alarm systems with kill switches are forcing car thieves to switch over to carjacking. You can protect yourself by becoming familiar with the methods, ruses, and locations commonly used by carjackers.

Avoidance (Alert Mode)

The first step is to avoid an attack. Be in Alert Mode at all times and be aware of your environment. The most likely places for a carjacking are:

- High crime areas

- Less-traveled roads (rural areas)

- Intersections where you must stop

- Isolated areas in parking lots

- Residential driveways and gates

- Traffic jams or congested areas

Learn to avoid these areas and situations, if possible. If not, take steps to prevent an attack by following this protocol:

- In traffic, look around for possible avenues of escape. Keep some distance between your car and the vehicle in front of you—about one-half of your vehicle's length—so you can maneuver easily if necessary. (You should always be able to see the rear tires of the vehicle in front of you. Tailgating isn't just rude, it cuts off your own options.)

- When stopped, use your rear and side view mirrors to stay aware of your surroundings. Keep your doors locked and windows up. This increases your safety and makes it more difficult for an attacker to surprise you.

Accidents are one ruse used by attackers as a prelude to a carjacking. The following are other common attack plans:

The Bump. The attacker bumps the victim's vehicle from behind. The victim gets out to assess the damage and exchange information. The victim's vehicle is then taken.

The "Bump"

1. Attacker "bumps" victim

2. Victim gets out and checks for damages

3. Attacker steals vehicle

Good Samaritan. The attacker(s) stage what appears to be an accident. They may simulate an injury. The victim stops to assist, and the vehicle is taken. (As you'll recall, this ruse was attempted on me in Africa.)

The "Good Samaritan"

1. Attacker signals they are in trouble

2. Victim offers assistance

3. Attacker steals victim's vehicle

The Ruse. The vehicle behind the victim flashes its lights or the driver waves to get the victim's attention. The attacker tries to indicate that there is a problem with the victim's car. The victim pulls over, and the vehicle is taken.

The "Ruse"

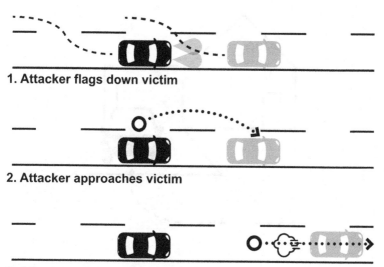

1. Attacker flags down victim

2. Attacker approaches victim

3. Attacker steals victim's vehicle

The Trap. Carjackers use surveillance to follow the victim home. When the victim pulls into his or her driveway waiting for the gate to open, the attacker pulls up from behind and blocks the victim's car.

The "Trap"

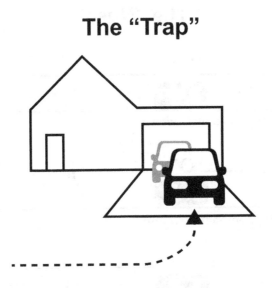

- If you are bumped from behind or if someone tries to alert you to a problem with your vehicle, pull over only when you reach a safe public place.

- If you are driving into a gated community, call ahead to have the gate opened. Otherwise, wait on the street until the gate is open before turning in and possibly getting trapped between the gate and a car behind you.

- Think before stopping to assist in an accident. It may be safer to call and report the location, number of cars involved, and any injuries you observed, rather than getting out of your car to offer your help.

- You can avoid becoming a victim. Ruses and methods, as well as the types of cars most often targeted, differ from country to country. Talk with the regional security officer (RSO) at your embassy about local scams and accident procedures.

- In all cases, keep your cell phone with you, and immediately alert someone about your situation.

During a Carjacking (Crisis Mode)

In most carjacking situations, the attackers are interested only in the vehicle. Try to stay calm. Do not stare at the attacker, as this may seem aggressive and cause them to harm you.

There are two options during an attack: nonresistive/nonconfrontational behavior or resistive/confrontational behavior. Your reaction should be based on certain factors:

- Type of attack: is it confrontational or is it calm and professional?

- Environment (isolated or public)

- Mental state of attacker (reasonable or nervous)

- Number of attackers

- Weapons

- The presence of children

In a nonconfrontational situation, you would:

- Give up the vehicle freely.

- Listen carefully to all directions.

- Make no quick or sudden movements that could be construed as a counterattack.

- Always keeps your hands in plain view.

- Tell the attacker of every move in advance.

- Make the attacker aware if children are present. The attacker may be focused only on the driver and not know children are in the car.

- Check your attacker's appearance (without staring). Try to note height, weight, scars or other distinguishing marks, hair and eye color, the presence of facial hair, build (slender, large), and complexion (dark, fair).

- If possible, get the license number, color, make, model, and year of the attacker's vehicle, as well as any marks (scratches, dents, damage) and personal decorations (stickers, colored wheels).

In a resistive or confrontational response, you would make a decision to escape or attack the carjacker. Before doing so, consider:

- The mental state of the attacker. If he's nervous, don't mirror his behavior. If he's confrontational and yelling, don't match his volume. You want to calm the situation down. Aim to de-escalate, but be ready to take action if/when you need to.

- Possible avenues of escape.

- The number of attackers. There is usually more than one, and if you're outnumbered, you're likely to get injured or worse.

- The use of weapons. (Weapons are used in the majority of carjacking situations.)

- In most instances, it is probably safest to give up your vehicle. It's a rental!

Calm

In any threatening situation, keep cycling through these stages, and they will get you through.

C is for remain Calm above everything else. Project calm even if you're scared as hell inside.

A is for pay Attention. Be aware of the people with you, your captors, your surroundings, and the responses of all of the above to stimulation.

L is for Listen. Listen to their words and to what they're saying. Do as they ask and give calm, neutral responses. People who act out want to feel heard—so let them know you hear them.

M is for Managing. It's about managing yourself and your responses, and managing where you are in a situation. Can you maneuver your way toward an exit? Can you orient yourself so that you are in a less-threatening position?

After the Attack (Pre-Crisis)

- OODA loop other possible threats.

- If you are in a populated area, immediately go to a safe place.

- Once you are in a safe location, report the incident.

Reporting the Crime

- Describe the event. What time of day did it occur? Where did it happen? How did it happen? Who was involved?

- Describe the attacker(s).

- Describe the attacker's vehicle.

- The golden rule for descriptions is to give only that information you absolutely remember. If you are not sure, don't guess!

Kidnappings

Top places for kidnappings:

1. New Zealand

2. Pakistan

3. Luxembourg

4. Germany

5. Ecuador

6. Portugal

7. Cabo Verde

8. Netherlands

9. Bahamas

10. Morocco

Kidnapping is a low-risk, high-return business that is becoming increasingly common. Kidnappings can take place in public areas where someone may force you quietly by gunpoint into a vehicle. Or they can take place at a hotel or residence, where an assailant uses a weapon to force your cooperation in leaving the premises and entering a vehicle.

Express kidnappings are becoming more popular and have increasingly been seen as a method used by taxi drivers. These kidnappings only last an hour or more, and generally involve forcing the victim to withdraw money from ATM machines.

The initial phase of kidnapping is a critical one as it provides one of the best opportunities to escape. If you are in a public area at the time of abduction, make as much commotion as possible to draw attention to the situation. If the abduction takes place at your hotel room, make noise and attempt to arouse the suspicion or concern of hotel employees or of those in neighboring rooms. At the least, the fact that an abduction has taken place will be brought to the attention of authorities, and the process of notification and search can begin. Otherwise, it could be hours or days before your absence is reported.

Once you have been forced into a vehicle, you may be blindfolded, physically attacked (to cause unconsciousness), drugged, or forced to lie face down on the floor of the vehicle. In some instances, hostages have been forced into trunks or specially built compartments for transporting contraband.

Do not struggle in your confined state. Calm yourself mentally and concentrate on surviving.

Employ your mind by attempting to visualize the route being taken, taking note of turns, street noise, smells, etc. Try to keep track of the amount of time spent between points.

Once you have arrived at your destination, you may be placed in a temporary holding area before being moved again to a more permanent detention site.

If You Are Interrogated:

- Retain a sense of pride but be cooperative.

- Divulge only information that cannot be used against you.

- Do not antagonize your interrogator with obstinate behavior.

- Concentrate on surviving. If you are to be used as a bargaining tool or to obtain ransom, you will be kept alive.

- After reaching what you may presume to be your permanent detention site (you may be moved several more times), quickly settle into the situation.

- Be observant. Notice the details of the room and the sounds of activity in the building, and determine the layout of the building by studying what is visible to you. Listen for sounds coming through walls or windows, or out in the streets. Try to distinguish between smells.

- Stay mentally active by memorizing the aforementioned details. Exercise your memory and practice retention.

- Keep track of time. Devise a way to track the date and the time, and use it to devise a daily schedule of activities for yourself.

- Know your captors. Memorize their schedule, look for patterns of behavior to be used to your advantage, and identify weaknesses or vulnerabilities.

- Use all of the above information to seek opportunities to escape.

- Remain cooperative. Attempt to establish rapport with your captors or guards. Once a level of communication is achieved, try asking for items that will increase your personal comfort. Make them aware of your needs.

- Stay physically active even if your movement is extremely limited. Use isometric and flexing exercises to keep your muscles toned.

- If you detect the presence of other hostages in the same building, devise ways to communicate.

- DO NOT be uncooperative, antagonistic, or hostile toward your captors. Hostages who display this type of behavior are frequently kept captive longer and may be singled out for torture or punishment.

- Watch for signs of Stockholm Syndrome, which occurs when the captive, because of close proximity and the constant pressures involved, begins to relate to, and empathize with, the captors. In some cases, the hostage becomes empathetic to the point that he or she actively participates in the activities of the group. You should attempt to establish a friendly rapport with your captors, but maintain your personal values and do not compromise your integrity.

- If you are able to escape, attempt to get first to a US Embassy or Consulate to seek protection. If you cannot reach either, go to a host government or friendly government entity.

Hostage Situations

Any traveler could become a hostage. The odds of that happening are extremely low—there are far more people who have traveled safely than those who have traveled and been taken hostage. That said, there is always that slim chance that a traveler could end up being in the wrong place at the wrong time. With this in mind, the traveler should make sure that his or her affairs are in order before going abroad. Items of particular importance to an individual in a hostage situation include an up-to-date will, insurance policy, and power of attorney for a spouse, if applicable. If these items have been taken care of before departure, the individual will not have to worry about their family's welfare, and the hostage can focus all of his or her efforts on the one thing of paramount importance—SURVIVAL!

Travelers must realize that there are certain dynamics involved in a hostage situation or a kidnapping, and that these dynamics interact with each other, with an impact on the end result. One wrong move by either a victim or a perpetrator could easily result in a disaster rather than a peaceful conclusion to the incident.

The first thing a traveler should remember is that he or she is not the only one who is scared and nervous. Everyone involved is in the same emotional state, including the perpetrators. Fear can trigger a disaster, and it does not take much to set off a defensive spate of violence in some individuals. This violence could be intended to reinforce a demand or to incite fear in the minds of the hostages. Whether the violence is motivated by fanaticism or fear, the hostage-takers will direct that violence at the person(s) perceived to be a threat or a nuisance.

211

The guidelines below will help you minimize the possibility of being selected for special attention by the perpetrators and maximize your ability to survive a hostage situation.

Hijacking Survival Guidelines

The physical takeover of any sort of public transportation, whether it's a train, a bus, a car, or an airplane, may be characterized by noise, commotion, and possibly shooting and yelling. Or, it may be quiet and methodical, characterized by little more than an announcement by a crew member. The first few minutes of the hijacking are crucial, and you should try to:

- Stay calm and encourage others around you to do the same.

- Remember that the hijackers are extremely nervous and are possibly scared.

- Comply with your captor(s)' directions.

- If shooting occurs, keep your head down or drop to the floor.

- Remain alert.

- Be ready to kill the hijackers if possible.

Once the takeover of the transport has occurred, you may be separated by citizenship, sex, race, and so on. Your passport may be confiscated and your carry-on luggage ransacked. The hijackers may enter into a negotiation phase, which could last for what seems like an indefinite period of time. In addition, the transport may be forced to divert to another destination.

During this phase, passengers may be used as a bargaining tool in negotiations, lives may be threatened, or a number of passengers may be released in exchange for items like fuel, landing/departure rights, or food. This will be the longest phase of the hijacking, and you should keep the following in mind:

- Prepare yourself mentally and emotionally for a long ordeal.

- If you are told to keep your head down or maintain another body position, talk yourself into relaxing into the position. You may need to stay that way for some time.

- Do not attempt to hide your passport or belongings.

- If addressed by the hijackers, respond in a calm tone of voice.

- Use your time wisely by observing the characteristics and behavior of the hijackers, mentally attach nicknames to each one, and notice their dress, facial features, and temperaments.

- If you or nearby passengers are in need of assistance because of illness or discomfort, solicit the assistance of a crew member first. Do not attempt to approach a hijacker unless similar assistance has been rendered by them for other passengers.

- If the hijackers single you out, be responsive but do not volunteer information.

The last phase of the hijacking is resolution. This may occur through a hostage rescue team or a negotiation. In the latter instance, the hijackers may simply surrender to authorities or abandon the transport, crew, and passengers. In the case of a hostage rescue operation, you may experience a similar situation as when the transport was taken over by the hijackers. There will be noise, chaos, and possibly shooting as the rescue force regains control. During this time of jeopardy, you should take care and remember the following:

- If you hear shots fired inside or outside the transport, immediately assume a protective position. Put your head down or drop to the floor.

- If instructed by a rescue force to move, do so quickly. Put your hands up in the air or behind your head. Make no sudden movements.

- If fire or smoke appears, attempt to get emergency exits open.

- Follow the instructions of the rescue force or local authorities. If neither is there to guide you, move as quickly as possible away from the transport.

- Expect to be regarded initially as a hijacker or coconspirator by the rescue force. You will be treated roughly until it is determined by the rescue force that you are not part of the hijacking team.

- Cooperate with local authorities and members of the US Embassy, Consulate, or other US agencies in relating information about the hijacking.

- Your contact with family members and travel going forward will be arranged by US authorities as soon as possible.

September 11 changed views on hijacking considerably. Could such an act happen again? Sure, but it's not likely. If it seems like a suicide mission is unfolding, then OODA loop the situation and become the wolf.

ENVIRONMENTAL THREATS

Environmental threats overseas are no different than such threats in the United States. The infrastructure and warning systems of other countries, however, are dramatically different. Buildings, dams, piers, communication systems, advanced warning systems, media, and other forms of protection and communication are frequently subpar, to say the least, and that's all without taking into account the issue of language barriers. As a result of these deficiencies, natural disasters and other types of environmental threats are even more of a risk abroad than they are at home. You may not know about incoming storm systems until they are literally on top of you. Once again, you should conduct a country study before departure to identify potential environmental threats and specifics, such as frequency of weather incidents, active seasons or areas, and actions to take.

Hurricane/Typhoon

If a hurricane or typhoon suddenly appears:

- Language permitting, listen to the radio or TV for information.

- Secure your location, close storm shutters, and secure outdoor objects or bring them indoors.

- Turn off utilities if instructed to do so. Otherwise, turn the refrigerator thermostat to its coldest setting and keep its doors closed.

- Turn off propane tanks.

- Avoid using the phone except for serious emergencies.

- Ensure a supply of water for sanitary purposes, such as cleaning and flushing toilets. Fill the bathtub and other large containers with water.

You should evacuate under the following conditions:

- If you are directed by local authorities to do so. Be sure to follow their instructions.

- If you are in a high-rise building. High winds are stronger at higher elevations.

- If you are on the coast, on a floodplain, near a river, or on an inland waterway.

- If you feel you are in danger, you probably are.

If you are unable to evacuate, follow these guidelines:

- Stay indoors and away from windows and glass doors during the hurricane/typhoon.

- Close all interior doors and secure and brace external doors.

- Keep curtains and blinds closed.

- Do not be fooled if there is a lull. If it's the eye of the storm, winds will pick up again.

- Take refuge in a small interior room, closet, or hallway on the lowest level.

- Lie on the floor under a table or another sturdy object.

Tsunami

If you are in a coastal area with a history of earthquakes, a tsunami is always a possibility. Warnings by radio or television or witnessed seismic activity should be taken very seriously, regardless of the population's actions. If there is noticeable recession in water away from the shoreline, this is Mother Nature's warning to you to move to higher ground. Do it quickly.

The 2004 Indian Ocean earthquake was an undersea earthquake that occurred the day after Christmas. That earthquake triggered the most devastating tsunami in recorded history. More than 225,000 people lost their lives in eleven countries. Indonesia, Sri Lanka, India, and Thailand were hit hardest by the one-hundred-foot waves. A warning system could have saved thousands of lives. Lives could still have been saved had the warnings by Mother Nature been recognized and heeded.

Don't Be a "Mr. Atala"

Like everyone else in Maullin, Chile, Ramon Atala survived the 1960 Chile earthquake. Mr. Atala was Maullin's most prosperous merchant. Outside of town, he owned a barn and a plantation of Monterey pine. In town, he owned a pier and at least one large building, and he also had private quarters in a waterfront warehouse. When a tsunami struck Maullin after the earthquake, Mr. Atala ventured to his warehouse to retrieve something; he left after the first wave, but before the second. When the second wave of the tsunami hit (yes, there are several waves), Mr. Atala's warehouse was washed away, and his body was never found. It is unclear what he was trying to save. What is clear is that no possession is worth your life. It is important to get to higher ground away from the coast and stay there until you are sure it is safe to return.

Winter Storm

Some of us are familiar with winter storms, but depending on where you live, you may have little to no experience with them. You are often most vulnerable to unexpected weather when driving, especially in a foreign country.

If stranded in a snowstorm:

- Pull off the highway. Turn on your hazard lights and hang a distress flag from the radio antenna or window.

- Remain in your vehicle where rescuers are most likely to find you.

- Do not set out on foot unless you can see a building close by where you know you can take shelter. Be careful. Distances are distorted by blowing snow. A building may seem close, but in reality it may be too far to walk to in deep snow.

- Run the engine and heater for about ten minutes of each hour to keep warm. When the engine is running, open a downwind window slightly for ventilation and periodically clear snow from the exhaust pipe. This will protect you from possible carbon monoxide poisoning.

- Exercise to maintain body heat but avoid overexertion. In extreme cold, use road maps, seat covers, and floor mats for insulation. Huddle with passengers and use your coat for a blanket.

- If you have a companion, take turns sleeping. One person should be awake at all times to look for rescue crews.

- Drink fluids to avoid dehydration.

- Be careful not to waste battery power. Balance electrical energy needs—the use of lights, heat, and radio—with supply.

- Turn on the inside light at night so work crews or rescuers can see you.

- If stranded in a remote area, stomp large block letters in an open area spelling out HELP or SOS and line with rocks or tree limbs to attract the attention of rescue personnel who may be surveying the area by airplane.

- Leave the car and proceed on foot, if necessary, once the blizzard passes.

Structural Fire

Fire safety, at home and abroad, is a matter of thinking ahead, knowing what to do, and keeping your fear under control. Panic and smoke are the most dangerous threats in the case of a fire. To minimize the risk of being trapped during a fire, the traveler should remember the precautions listed below when feasible:

- Stay only at hotels with smoke detectors and/ or sprinklers installed in all rooms. The hotel should provide information about fire and safety procedures.

- Request a room between the second and seventh floor. Most fire departments do not have the capability to rescue people above the seventh floor level with ladder rescue equipment.

- Ask the hotel desk clerk how guests are notified if there is an emergency.

Your hotel room:

- Note the location of the fire exits (stairs) on your floor. Count the number of doors between your room and the exit. If there is a fire, you may have to crawl there in the dark.

- Check exit doors to be sure that they are unlocked and that stairwells are clear of obstructions.

- Note the location of fire alarms, extinguishers, and hoses. Read any fire safety information available in your room.

- Check outside your room window to ascertain if there is a possible escape route that would be feasible in an extreme emergency.

In case of a fire:

- KEEP CALM. DO NOT PANIC.

- Call the front desk and notify them of the location of the fire, if you know.

- Check your door by placing your palm on the door and then on the doorknob. If either feels hot, DO NOT OPEN THE DOOR.

- If it is safe to exit from your room, head for the stairs. Take your room key with you, as you may have to return to your room.

- If the corridor is full of smoke, crawl to the exit. Again, check the exit door before opening it to see if it is hot. The fire could be in the stairwell.

- DO NOT USE THE ELEVATOR.

If you cannot leave your room, or if the stairwells are unsafe and you must return to your room:

- Notify the front desk that you are in your room waiting to be rescued.

- Open a window for fresh air. Do not break the window as you may need to close it again if smoke starts to enter from the outside.

- Fill the tub and sink with water. Soak towels and blankets as necessary to block vents and openings around doors to keep the smoke and fumes out.

- Attempt to keep the walls, doors, and cracks covered with towels that are cool and wet.

- A wet towel swung around the room will help clear the air of smoke.

- Cover your mouth and nose with a wet cloth.

- Stay low, but alert to any signs of rescue from the street or the halls. Let the firefighters know where you are by waving a towel or sheet out the window.

An excellent resource for fire-safety information is the National Fire Protection Association (NFPA), an international nonprofit organization that provides guidance on fire, electrical and building codes, and fire safety education and research.

AGENCY THREATS

When I say Agencies, I'm referring to any body of people who are relatively organized. So that could be foreign intelligence services, law enforcement, terrorist groups, organized crime, etc. Intelligence and law enforcement agencies are always considered a threat, regardless of whether they are hostile or not. This includes the agencies that belong to the country you're visiting *and* agencies of other countries that may be operating there, as well. If you're a businessperson and think they want nothing to do with you, think again. In today's globalized economy and advanced technology, country borders are nonexistent in the business world. National intelligence and law enforcement agencies are playing bigger and bigger roles in corporate espionage, which is a precursor to economic espionage. And it doesn't take long before economic espionage morphs into sabotage.

This isn't something most people think about. Agencies are an invisible threat, but they are always there. In the US, we are used to thinking of law enforcement (whether that's the local PD, the FBI, or anything else) as being on our side, but that may not always be the case in a foreign country. How does this country view a US citizen? How does it view its own citizens? Is the law enforcement there effective?

The people you think of as "the good guys" may not always be. Be cautious with foreign law enforcement. For instance, you may follow the rules of the road and still get pulled over, because they're looking for bribes. That does happen.

But how do you know that's what's going on? I've missed plenty of stop signs without realizing it, and it's obviously best not to assume the resulting traffic stop is a shakedown. So how to manage this? You don't want to just hand over some money to a foreign police officer, or say something like, "Do I need to pay you money to get out of this?" They might put you in jail for attempted bribery. It's a balancing act, but one you can manage by having done your research on local law enforcement customs before traveling.

Regardless, there is a graceful way to handle this kind of situation. If you're asked to show your credentials, just pull out some cash and put it on the dashboard of your car. Then look the other way—pretend that cash doesn't exist. There's no evidence you're trying to bribe someone, so you can't get in trouble for it. Let the situation dictate itself. If they take the money and let you go on your merry way, great. If all they do next is give you a ticket, leaving the cash in place, that's fine, too.

TERRORISM THREATS

The key factors that spawned international terrorism show no signs of abating over the next fifteen years...Lagging economies, ethnic affiliations, intense religious convictions, and youth bulges will align to create a "perfect storm," creating conditions likely to spawn internal conflict. The governing capacity of states, however, will determine whether and to what extent conflicts actually occur. Those states unable both to satisfy the expectations of their peoples and to resolve or quell conflicting demands among them are likely to encounter the most severe and most frequent outbreaks of violence. (National Intelligence Council)

Terrorism feeds on global discontent with the United States and allows potential terrorists to commit to destroying themselves in the name of a cause or religion. This is true all over the world, and terrorism has been going on for centuries. It's here to stay.

That said, it may look different depending on where you go. According to the National Advisory Committee on Criminal Justice Standards and Goals, there are six distinct types of terrorism:

1. **Civil disorder.** A sometimes violent form of protest held by a group of individuals, usually in opposition to a political policy or action. The protest is intended to be nonviolent, but can sometimes result in large riots in which private property is destroyed and civilians are injured or killed.

2. **Political terrorism.** Used by one political faction to intimidate or overthrow another, often by attacking citizens with violence.

3. **Nonpolitical terrorism.** A terrorist act perpetrated by a group for any other purpose, most often of a religious nature. The desired goal isn't a political objective, but the tactics involved are the same.

4. **Quasi terrorism.** A violent act that utilizes the same methods terrorists employ, but does not have the same motivating factors. Cases like this usually involve an armed criminal who is trying to escape from law enforcement taking civilians as hostages to help them escape. The law breaker is acting in a similar manner to a terrorist, but terrorism is not the goal.

5. **Limited political terrorism.** Acts are generally one-time-only plots to make a political or ideological statement. The goal is not to overthrow the government, but to protest a governmental policy or action.

6. **State terrorism.** Defines any violent action initiated by an existing government to achieve a particular goal. Most often this goal involves a conflict with another country.

Every type of terrorism uses violence to get their message across. That can mean anything from assault weapons or explosive devices to airborne toxins. These attacks may occur at any time or place, which makes them an extremely effective method of instilling terror and uncertainty into the general public.

It's important to study which terrorist organizations exist along your route overseas and at your destination. These can change quickly, so following the political and economic situations around the world (not just in the US) will help you understand the dynamics and risks of the countries you visit.

Myth vs. Reality

- **MYTH.** Poverty is the primary breeding ground for terrorism.

- **Reality.** Many terrorists come from middle-class families and typically have college degrees. Most of their degrees are in the technical sciences and engineering. Terrorists really have no common ground other than motivation.

- **MYTH.** US foreign policy drives radicalization.

- **Reality.** Radicalization usually stems from local frustrations caused by international events. Radicalization causes are diverse and vary by location and group.

- **MYTH.** All terrorists are Muslim.

- **Reality.** Terrorists' motivations are vast. There are hundreds of terrorist organizations that use the same tactics for a variety of reasons. The motivations, just to list a few, include religion, nationalism, anarchism, Leftism, communism, Leninism, Maoism, Marxism, ethnic terrorism (which includes neo-Nazis and white supremacists), anti-communism, Cuban exile groups, and issue-specific groups (like eco-terrorists and anti-abortion extremists).

Terrorist-Specific Tactics

Bioterrorism. A bioterrorism attack is the deliberate release of viruses, bacteria, or other germs (agents) to cause illness or death in people, animals, or plants. These agents are typically found in nature, but sometimes altered to increase their ability to cause disease, make them resistant to current medicines, or further their spread into the environment. Biological agents can be spread through air, water, or food.

Terrorists may use biological agents because they can be extremely difficult to detect and do not cause illness for several hours to several days. Some bioterrorism agents, like the smallpox virus, can be spread from person to person. Some, like anthrax, cannot.

Suicide Bombers. In a suicide attack upon a target, the attacker intends to kill others and cause great damage, knowing that he or she will either certainly, or most likely, die in the process. These attacks can use explosive-laden vests, vehicles, aircraft, or vessels. Although recent history has focused on Muslims and their individual quests to martyrdom, these tactics have been going on since the beginning of time. Just eighty years ago, the Japanese were using submarines and aircraft (*kaiten* and *kamikaze*) to cause the same effects. One group does it for God and possible rewards in the afterlife, and the other for honor and country.

Alerting signs of a suicide bomber:

Alerting Signs of a Suicide Bomber:

· Tunnel vision

· Intense stare

· Poor projection

· Clothing may not match season

· A visible vest hidden under clothing

· Exposed wires or trigger in hand

· Mumbling or rambling in prayer

If you see signs of a possible suicide bomber, make it known. Take cover. And pray for a dud.

Beheadings. Muslim terror groups use beheadings not only for the fear factor, but also to fulfill their interpretation of the Quran. For centuries, leading Islamic scholars have interpreted this verse literally. The famous Iranian histo-rian and Quran commentator Muhammad, b. Jarir at-Tabari (d. 923 C.E.), wrote that "striking at the necks" is simply God's sanction of ferocious opposition to non-Muslims. Mahmud, b. Umar az-Zamakhshari (d. 1143 C.E.), in a major commentary studied for centuries by Sunni religious schol-ars, suggested that any prescription to "strike at the necks" commands to avoid striking elsewhere so as to confirm death and not simply wound. The practice of beheading non-Mus-lim captives extends back to the Prophet himself. Ibn Ishaq (d. 768 C.E.), the earliest biographer of Muhammad, is recorded as saying that the Prophet ordered the execution by decapitation of 700 men of the Jewish Banu Qurayza tribe in Medina for allegedly plotting against him. Islamic leaders from Muhammad's time have followed his model. Examples of decapitation, of both the living and the dead, in Islamic history are myriad.

The Dirty Bomb. A dirty bomb is a mix of explosives, such as dynamite with radioactive powder or pellets. When the dynamite or other explosives are set off, the blast carries radioactive material into the surrounding area. A dirty bomb is *not* the same as an atomic bomb. An atomic bomb, like the bombs dropped on Hiroshima and Nagasaki, Japan, involves the splitting of atoms and a huge release of energy, which produces an atomic mushroom cloud.

A dirty bomb works completely differently and *cannot create an atomic blast*. Instead, a dirty bomb uses dynamite or other explosives to scatter radioactive dust, smoke, or other material and cause radioactive contamination.

What Are the Main Dangers of a Dirty Bomb?

The main danger from a dirty bomb is from the explosion, which can cause serious injuries and property damage. The radioactive materials used in a dirty bomb would probably not create enough radiation exposure to cause immediate serious illness, except for individuals who are very close to the blast site. As the radioactive dust and smoke spreads farther away, it could be dangerous if inhaled. Because you cannot see, smell, feel, or taste radiation, you should take immediate steps to protect yourself and your loved ones.

What Immediate Actions Should You Take to Protect Yourself?

These simple steps, recommended by doctors and radiation experts, will help protect you. What actions you take depend on where you are located when the incident occurs—outside, inside, or in a vehicle.

If you are outside and close to the incident:

- Cover your nose and mouth with a cloth to reduce the risk of breathing in radioactive dust or smoke.

- Don't touch objects thrown off by an explosion. They might be radioactive.

- Quickly go into a building where the walls and windows have not been broken. This area will shield you from radiation that might be outside.

- Once you are inside, take off your outer layer of clothing and seal it in a plastic bag if available. Put the cloth you used to cover your mouth in the bag, too. Removing outer clothes may get rid of up to 90 percent of radioactive dust.

- Put the plastic bag where others will not touch it and keep it until authorities tell you what to do with it.

- Shower or wash with soap and water. Be sure to wash your hair. Washing will remove any remaining dust.

- Tune to the local radio or television news for more instructions.

If you are inside and close to the incident:

- If the walls and windows of the building are not broken, stay in the building and do not leave.

- To keep radioactive dust or powder from getting

inside, shut all windows, outside doors, and fireplace dampers. Turn off fans and heating and air-conditioning systems that bring in air from the outside. It is not necessary to put duct tape or plastic around doors or windows.

- If the walls and windows of the building are broken, go to an interior room and do not leave. If the building has been heavily damaged, quickly go into a building where the walls and windows have not been broken. If you must go outside, be sure to cover your nose and mouth with a cloth. Once you are inside, take off your outer layer of clothing and seal it in a plastic bag if available. Store the bag where others will not touch it.

- Shower or wash with soap and water, removing any remaining dust. Be sure to wash your hair.

- Tune to local radio or television news for more instructions.

If you are in a car when the incident happens:

- Close the windows and turn off the air conditioner, heater, and vents.

- Cover your nose and mouth with a cloth to avoid breathing radioactive dust or smoke.

- If you are close to your home, office, or a public building, go there immediately and go inside quickly.

- If you cannot get to your home or another building safely, pull over to the side of the road and stop in the safest place possible. If it is a hot or sunny day, try to stop under a bridge or in a shady spot.

- Turn off the engine and listen to the radio for instructions.

- Stay in the car until you are told it is safe to get back on the road.

Will food and water supplies be safe?

- Food and water supplies most likely will remain safe. Any unpackaged food or water out in the open and close to the incident may have radioactive dust on it. Therefore, do not consume water or food that was out in the open.

- The food inside of cans and other sealed containers will be safe to eat. Wash the outside of the container before opening it.

How do I know if I've been exposed to radiation or contaminated by radioactive materials?

- People cannot see, smell, feel, or taste radiation. So you may not know whether you have been exposed. Police or firefighters will quickly check for radiation by using special equipment to determine how much radiation is present and whether it poses any danger in your area.

Low levels of radiation exposure (like those expected from a dirty bomb situation) do not cause any symptoms. Higher levels of radiation exposure may produce symptoms, such as nausea, vomiting, diarrhea, and swelling and redness of the skin. If you develop any of these symptoms, you should contact your doctor, hospital, or other sites recommended by authorities.

> *"There are only two emotions in a plane: boredom and terror."*
>
> —ORSON WELLES

WHAT DOES THIS MEAN?

The odds of all of these happening to any one person are obviously pretty slim. But the fact that there *is* so much to be aware of means that you'll probably face at least one or two of these challenges in your lifetime. Be informed, be prepared, and be safe.

CHAPTER 6 REVIEW

PRACTICE ASSIGNMENT— THREATS

WHEN PREPARATION PAYS OFF

IN THIS CHAPTER, WE'VE EXPLORED THE VARIOUS TYPES OF ENVIRONMENtal threats. Some are natural, and some are manmade. All can be lethal if you aren't prepared to avoid or minimize the risks associated with them. It's a matter of proper preparation before you even pick up your suitcase. When traveling, you then need to practice good Situational Awareness, Personal Awareness, and Third-Party Awareness.

Now let's see how to apply those skills to a hypothetical situation.

PRACTICAL EXAMPLE

- Semi-permissive environment (area with some government control)

- Vacationing in a popular resort area in a remote area of Greece

You recently arrived at a nice resort area and checked into your bungalow. Just as you step out into the sun, you feel a tremor. The shaking doesn't stop for what seems like an eternity. The wood in your bungalow starts to creak, and rocks from the nearby cliffs start to tumble. People run out into the streets, screaming. Then suddenly, everything is quiet. You've just gone through a major earthquake. There's no electricity, no services, no transportation. A number of people in the local community have been hurt or killed. You're lucky to have come through without injury. But what do you do now?

STUDY GUIDE QUESTIONS

What preparations could you have made before beginning your trip that would have helped you cope with a disaster scenario?

How will you find food, water, and shelter until you can identify a way to leave the scene of the disaster?

STUDY GUIDE ANSWERS

What preparations could you have made before beginning your trip that would have helped you cope with a disaster scenario?

Before leaving home, you had the foresight to educate yourself about the overall environment and the types of threats that were present. In this case, while thoroughly researching your lovely resort area, you came across the information that Greece is one of the world's most seismically active countries. Although most Greek earthquakes are mild, there is always the potential for more severe seismic activity.

You took steps to register with the US Embassy in Greece, so the government would know you were at the resort. You also signed up for the US Geological Survey's earthquake notification service and had text notifications sent to your cell phone (which you checked to make sure it would work in Greece). As a result, you learned of a few earlier, smaller tremors. So you weren't totally unprepared.

How would you find food, water, and shelter until you can identify a way to leave the scene of the disaster?

You are carrying a list of emergency contact numbers, including local emergency services, hospitals, and embassies or consulates. Since you don't speak Greek, you have a list of emergency words and phrases that will come in very handy when asking for assistance, food, and water.

You have taken time to scope out shelter in your hotel room, the exterior area, and an evacuation route for after the earthquake. You have determined how to get to higher ground since you are staying near the ocean—just in case the earthquake triggered a tsunami.

It will be a challenging couple of days, but thanks to advance preparation and your ability to make good decisions in the moment, you will come through the incident unscathed.

NOTES:

_____

_____

_____

_____

_____

_____

_____

_____

_____

_____

_____

_____

_____

_____

_____

_____

_____

TRAVEL PREPARATION AND PLANNING

"A journey is like marriage. The certain way to be wrong is to think you control it."

—JOHN STEINBECK

BY NOW, YOU'RE WELL AWARE OF THE VARIOUS DIFFERENT WAYS THAT traveling professionals can become targets for criminal and terrorist attacks and environmental threats. But as you understand by now, there are important steps you can take to protect yourself *before* you travel. Based primarily on US State Department information, this chapter discusses security-conscious travel planning and preparation.

COUNTRY STUDY AND RESEARCH

It pays to use the Total Awareness System to plan out your trip from beginning to end. Personal, Cultural, Third-Party, and THREAT assessments must be done to increase your overall Situational Awareness. Know the environments (permissive, semi-permissive, or nonpermissive) and threats that you could potentially face. Understand the culture and adapt your Personal Awareness accordingly. Write out the THREAT acronym (see Chapter 6) on a piece of paper and look each of them up. Like G.I. Joe, "knowing is half the battle."

BEFORE YOU GO

Enroll in the **S**mart **T**raveler **E**nrollment **P**rogram (STEP). The STEP Program is a free service of the Bureau of Consular Affairs that allows US citizens and nationals traveling abroad to enroll their trip with the nearest US Embassy or Consulate. In other words, the US Embassy or Consulate in the country you are visiting will know that you are "in country" and can assist travelers in need. The STEP program helps travelers by:

- Providing important information from the Embassy about safety conditions in your destination country. This helps you make informed decisions about your travel plans.

- Helping the US Embassy contact you in an emergency, whether natural disaster, civil unrest, or family emergency.

- Helping family and friends get in touch with you in an emergency.

The US Department of State also developed a free Smart Traveler app that allows you to participate in the STEP program, receive alerts/warnings, and research specific country information all from your device.

Travel Itinerary

DO NOT publicize your travel plans. In this age of social media, this has become all the more important. Too many people want to post their travel plans on Facebook or other social media outlets, making themselves potential victims. Limit that knowledge to those who need to know. Leave a full itinerary of your travel schedule, hotel phone numbers, and business appointments with your office and with a family member or friend.

Passport

Is it valid and up to date? If not, you and everything in your possession may be looked at in-depth by host government

ESCAPE THE WOLF

authorities. If you are carrying documents that are sensitive or proprietary, they will be examined in detail to see if they reveal any interesting material. If they do, you can bet that copies will be made, and there will not be much that you can do about it.

Make photocopies of your passport, visa, and other important travel documents. Keep copies in both your carry-on and checked luggage. This makes it easier to replace your identification documents should anything happen to them. (It is also a good idea to leave a photocopy of these documents with someone at home.)

If your passport has the radio-frequency identification (RFID) symbol on the front, make sure you have some foil to wrap it up with, or enclose it in a case that blocks RFID readers and protects against identity theft.

Visas

Is a visa required for any of the countries you are visiting? Do you have the appropriate visa(s)? Is the information on your visa application true and correct? In some countries, falsifying information on a visa application can result in an unexpected vacation in the local bastilles.

Some countries are sensitive about the type of visa you obtain. If you are traveling on business, a business visa should be obtained. Otherwise, a tourist visa is acceptable.

Medical

Take an adequate supply of any needed prescription medication with you, as well as an extra set of eyeglasses or contact lenses. Also, take a copy of your eyeglasses and medical prescription(s) in case you should need to have anything replaced. Maintain your inoculation records and update them before each trip, as each country has different requirements.

Make a list of essential medical information—your blood type, allergies, medical conditions, and special requirements—and carry it with you. It is a good idea to wear a medical alert bracelet if you have a special medical condition.

Does the country you are visiting require any specific inoculations? Some countries require proof of vaccination for COVID-19, yellow fever, polio, and more. This information is available from embassies or consulates. Be sure to carry your international vaccination record, just in case.

If you do not have comprehensive medical coverage, consider enrolling in an international health program. Hospitals in foreign countries do not take credit cards and most will not honor US-based medical insurance plans.

Miscellaneous

- Consider obtaining a modest amount of foreign currency before you leave your home country. Criminals often watch for and target international travelers purchasing large amounts of foreign currency at airport banks and currency exchange windows.

- Carry only the documents you will need in your wallet/pocketbook. Take only the credit cards you plan to use on your trip.

- If you plan to rent a car, check to see if you must obtain an international driver's permit for the country you plan to visit.

- Obtain information from US Customs regarding any special requirements for the country you are visiting.

AT THE AIRPORT

To diminish the risks of turning from an innocent bystander into the victim of a terrorist attack or other criminal threats, there are a number of things you should remember when checking into an airport.

- In the event of a disturbance of any kind, go in the opposite direction. DO NOT GET INVOLVED.

- Plan to check in early for your flight to avoid long lines at the ticket counter.

- Go directly to the gate or secure zone after checking your luggage. (The secure zone is the area between security/immigration and the departure gate.) Avoid waiting rooms and shopping areas outside the secure areas.

- Stay away from glass-walled areas and airport coffee shops that are open to the concourse or public waiting areas.

- From the time you pack your luggage until you check it with the carrier at the airport, maintain positive control of all items, both hand-carried and checked.

- At many airports, security personnel, following Federal Aviation Administration (FAA) protocol, will ask you questions about control of your luggage. Know what items you are carrying and be able to describe all electrical items.

- When going through the pre-board screening process, cooperate with security personnel. Remember, they are there to help ensure that your travel is safe.

- When arriving at or departing from an airport, try not to exchange items between bags while waiting in line for security screening or immigration/customs processing. Complete all packing before entering such areas.

- If a conflict should arise while undergoing the screening process, cooperate. Obtain the names of the screeners involved. Then, discuss the matter with a supervisor from the appropriate air carrier.

- Remember that X-ray will not damage film, videos, or computer equipment. Many times such items can be cleared using X-ray, which avoids handling by the screener.

- Consider being transported to/from the airport by a hotel vehicle. Generally this transportation is free, and if not, the cost is not prohibitive, and arrangements can be made in advance.

- Declare all currency and other items as required by law.

- NEVER leave your luggage or briefcase unattended, even while checking in or in the secure zone. In some countries, the police or security forces assume that an unattended bag is a bomb, and your luggage could be forcefully opened or even destroyed.

- Always be aware of where you are in relation to where you are going. If an incident occurs, you need to know how to avoid it and get to where you need to go.

- Dress casually when traveling, as this will keep any undue attention from you. Once aboard the flight, remove your shoes for better circulation. Walk around the flight cabin from time to time to keep your blood circulating and minimize swelling.

- Avoid last-minute dashes to the airport.

- Eat moderately, avoid alcoholic beverages, and drink plenty of water as this will help to avoid dehydration.

- If possible, in the days before you leave, make an effort to adjust your sleep patterns.

- Sleep as much as possible during the flight.

- Carry airsickness medication with you. Even the best traveler sometimes experiences airsickness.

- Avoid a demanding schedule upon arrival. Give yourself a chance to adjust to your surroundings.

LOCAL IMPORT RESTRICTIONS

Request any lists or pamphlets describing customs restrictions or banned materials from the embassy of the country you plan to visit. This is designed to minimize the possibility of an encounter with the local authorities. Leave all expensive and heirloom jewelry at home.

LUGGAGE

- DO NOT pack sensitive or proprietary information in your checked luggage. Double-envelope sensitive material and hand carry it.

- Be sure that your luggage is tagged with covered tags that protect your address from open observation. Put your name and address inside each piece of luggage, and be sure that all luggage is locked or secured in some fashion. Avoid displaying your company's name or any logos on your luggage.

- DO NOT pack extra glasses or necessary daily medication in your luggage. Carry it in your briefcase, purse, or pocket. If your luggage is lost or you are the victim of a hijacking, you may need these items.

- Check with the airline and/or your personal insurance company regarding any lost luggage coverage.

- Make sure you use sturdy luggage. Do not over-pack, as the luggage could open if dropped. Bind the luggage with strapping to keep it intact.

- Never place valuables (jewelry, money, and travelers checks) in your checked luggage.

- Never leave your bags unattended.

Luggage Locks

The locks on your luggage are really no more than a deterrent. For a professional thief or manipulator, no luggage lock is secure. However, if time is of the essence to the perpetrator, as it usually is when a crime is involved, here are a couple of suggestions that might deter surreptitious entry and/or theft:

- For added security on all luggage, run a strip of nylon filament tape around the suitcase to preclude its opening accidentally if dropped or mistreated by baggage handlers.

- For luggage and briefcases with two combination locks, reset the combination locks from the factory combination (000) to different combinations on each of the right and left locks.

- For luggage with single locks, set the lock on each piece of luggage with a different combination.

- A TSA-accepted luggage lock allows baggage screeners and security agents to open your suitcase for inspection using a universal master key. A number of manufacturers produce TSA-accepted locks, and they're sold under different brand names. The TSA requires the packaging to clearly state that the lock is accepted and recognized by the agency and may be opened by a TSA master key. When shopping for a TSA-accepted lock, look for the Travel Sentry or Safe Skies logo on the packaging. The Travel Sentry logo is a red diamond, and the Safe Skies mark is a black airplane.

AIRLINE SECURITY AND SEAT SELECTION

- Try to book a nonstop flight, as these have fewer takeoffs and landings and therefore fewer opportunities for something to go awry.

- Choose an airline with a good safety and on-time record.

- Try to make your stopovers in airports with a high security standard and good security screening.

- Try to fly wide-body planes. Hijackers tend to avoid these as they are loaded with too many passengers.

- Most travelers prefer an aisle seat. Choose a window or center seat. This will keep you away from hijackers and any action that may be happening in the aisle.

SELECTING A SECURE HOTEL

- Many US corporations have hotels abroad that are owned by local businessmen and staffed by local workers but managed by first-class US hoteliers. You can usually expect levels of safety and security consistent with US standards.

- Check with the regional security officer at the US Embassy for a list of hotels used by officials visiting the area.

Making Reservations

- Avoid travel agents, and instead make your own reservations as long as doing so is practical and consistent with company policies. The fewer people involved in your travel and lodging arrangements, the better.

- If traveling abroad, especially in politically sensitive areas, consider making reservations using your employer's street address, without identifying the company, and using your personal credit card. Again, the less known about your travel itinerary, and whom you represent, the better.

- If arriving after 6:00 p.m., ensure that reservations are guaranteed.

- Request information about parking arrangements if you plan on renting an automobile.

- Be aware that credit card information can be compromised. Always audit monthly credit card statements to ensure that unauthorized use has not been made of your account.

- Join the frequent traveler programs available through many hotels. These programs enable upgrades to executive or concierge floors where available. Be sure to advise the person taking reservations that you are a member and request an upgrade.

ARRIVING AT OR DEPARTING FROM THE HOTEL

- The most vulnerable part of your journey is any travel between the point of departure or arrival and your hotel. Do not linger or wander unnecessarily in the hotel's parking lot or indoor garage, or in public space around the hotel. Be on the alert for suspicious persons and behavior. Watch for distractions that are intentionally staged to set up a pickpocket, luggage theft, or purse snatch.

- Stay with your luggage until it is brought into the lobby or placed into the taxi or limo.

- Consider using the bellman. When your luggage is in the "care, custody, and control" of the hotel, the hotel is liable for your property. Protect claim checks. They are your evidence! Allow the bellman to open the room, turn lights on, and check the room to ensure that it is vacant and ready for your stay. Before dismissing the bellman, always inspect the door lock, locks on sliding glass doors, optical viewer, privacy latch or chain, guest room safes, deadbolt lock on interconnecting suite door, and telephone. If a discrepancy is found, request a room change.

- Keep in mind, though, that there are limits on liability created by states and countries to protect hoteliers. Personal travel documents, laptops, jewelry, and other valuables and sensitive documents exceeding $1,000 in value should be hand carried and personally protected.

- If you arrive by car, park as close to a hotel access point as possible and in a lighted area. Remove all property from the car interior and either take it with you or place it in the trunk. Avoid leaving valuables or personal documents in the glove compartment. Before leaving the security of the vehicle, take note of any suspicious persons or behavior.

- If using valet service, leave only the ignition key, and take all other keys with you. Oftentimes valets are not employees of the hotel and work for contract firms.

- Parking garages are difficult to secure. Avoid dimly lit garages that are not patrolled and do not have security telephones or intercoms.

- Female travelers should consider asking for an escort to their vehicles when parked in a lot or garage.

Registration

- In some countries, your passport may be temporarily held by the hotel for review by the police or other authorities. Obtain its return at the earliest possible time.

- Be aware of persons in the hotel lobby who may have unusual interest in your arrival.

- If carrying your luggage, keep it within view or touch. One recommendation is to position luggage against your leg during registration, and to place a briefcase or a purse on the desk or counter in front of you.

- Ground-floor rooms that open to a pool or beach area via sliding glass doors or windows are considered particularly vulnerable. Depending upon the situation, area, and security coverage, exercise a higher level of security if assigned a first-floor room, or request a change.

- Female travelers should request rooms away from elevator landings and stairwells. This will help prevent being caught by surprise by persons exiting the elevator or hiding in the stairwell.

- Ask where the nearest fire stairwell is located. Make a mental note on which direction you must turn and approximately how many steps there are to the closest fire stairwell. In the event of a fire, there is frequently dense smoke and no lighting.

- Also observe where the nearest house telephone is located in case of an emergency. Determine whether the telephone is configured in such a manner that anyone can dial a guest room directly, or whether the phone is connected to the switchboard. Most security-conscious hotels require a caller to identify whom they are attempting to telephone rather than providing a room number.

- Note how hotel staff is uniformed and identified. Many "pretext" crimes occur by persons misrepresenting themselves as hotel employees on house telephones to gain access to guest rooms. Avoid permitting a person into the guest room unless you have confirmed that the person is authorized to enter. This can be verified by using the optical viewer and by calling the front desk.

IN YOUR HOTEL

"All hotel rooms abroad are bugged for audio and visual surveillance." This statement, of course, is not true, but that is the premise under which you must operate in order to maintain an adequate level of security awareness while conducting business abroad. Many hotel rooms overseas *are* under surveillance. In those countries where intelligence services are very active, if you are a businessperson working for an American company of interest to the government or a government-sponsored competitor, everything that you do in that hotel room may be recorded and analyzed for possible vulnerabilities or for any useful information.

With that basic premise established, the following security tips will minimize potential risks.

Hotel Room Key

Keep it with you at all times. The two most common ways thieves and others determine if a person is in their hotel room is to look at the hotel room mail slot or keyboard or call the room on the house phone. If you do not answer the phone, that is one sign to thieves. But a much clearer signal is the sight of your room key in the mail slot, a visual sign that the coast is clear for a thief or anyone else who might be interested in searching your room and luggage.

Upon Arrival

Invest in a good map of the city. Mark significant points on the map, such as your hotel, embassies, and police stations. Study the map and make a mental note of alternative routes to your hotel or local office should your map become lost or stolen. Be aware of your surroundings. Look up and down the street before exiting a building.

Avoid jogging or walking in cities you are not familiar with. If you must jog, be aware of the traffic patterns when crossing public streets. (Joggers have been seriously injured by failing to understand local traffic conditions.)

Valuables

Valuables should be left at home. The rule of thumb is, if you neither want nor can afford to lose them, do not take them. If, however, you must carry valuables, the best way to protect them is to secure them in your local offices. If that is not possible, the next best course of action is to seal any valuables by double enveloping, initialing across seams, and taping all edges and seams before depositing them in the hotel's safe.

Luggage

Keep your luggage locked whenever you are out of the room. This measure will not stop the professional thief or intelligence agent, but it will keep the curious maid honest.

Passport

Keep your passport with you at all times. The only times that you should relinquish it are:

1. To the hotel if required by law when registering.

2. If you are required to identify yourself to local authorities for any reason.

At night, lock your passport and your other valuables in your luggage. This eliminates any mysterious disappearance while you are asleep or in the shower.

Use a portable or improvised burglar alarm while asleep. Two ashtrays and a water glass are quite effective as an alarm when placed on the floor in front of the entry door into your room. Place a water glass in one ashtray and put the second ashtray on top of the glass. If a straight chair is available, place it next to the door and put the ashtray/water glass alarm on the edge of the chair where it will fall with enough racket to wake you.

Guest Room as a "Safe Haven"

Hotels are required to provide reasonable care to ensure that guests have a safe and secure stay—but hotels are not required to guarantee guest security. Only you are responsible for your personal security and property. So, follow these precautions:

- While in the room, keep the door closed and engage the deadbolt and privacy latch or chain. Some hotel emergency keys can override the deadbolt locks. To ensure privacy, use the latch or chain!

- Hoteliers provide guest room "safes" for the convenience of guests. These containers, however, are not as durable as bank safes and can be breached.

Furthermore, Housekeepers Liability Laws provide that if guest property is not in the "care, custody. and control of the hotel," the hotel is not liable. Guests should always place money or valuables in the safe at the front desk of the hotel.

- When leaving the guest room, ensure that the door properly closes and is secured. Make a mental note of how your property was left. Avoid leaving valuables in plain view or in an unorganized manner. A number of hotel employees enter the room each day to clean, repair, and restock the room. Although the vast majority of hotel employees are honest and hardworking, a few succumb to the temptation of cash or jewelry left unprotected.

- If you determine that an item is missing, conduct a thorough search prior to reporting the incident to hotel security. Do not expect to receive a copy of the security report, as it is an internal document. The incident should be reported to the local police, the regional security, and consular officers at the US Embassy, as well as your insurance carrier. Hotel security can provide a letter verifying that you reported property missing.

- Prior to traveling, photocopy all credit cards, passport, air tickets, and other documents to facilitate reporting loss and replacing them. While traveling abroad, secure these documents in the room safe or in your locked luggage, and carry copies of your passport and visa.

- Request that housekeeping make up your room while you are at breakfast, rather than leaving a "Please Service This Room" sign on the doorknob. This sign is a signal to criminals that the room is unoccupied.

- If you are required to use parking stickers in your auto, be sure that they do not indicate your name or room number.

AROUND THE HOTEL

Most first-class international hotels spend a considerable sum to ensure your safety and security. Fire safety equipment, closed-circuit televisions (CCTVs), and security patrols are often part of the hotel's security plan. But regardless of the level of security provided by the hotel, you need to become familiar with certain aspects of the security profile of the hotel. This will take on increased significance if you are forced to stay at the only hotel at a particular location.

Vary the time and route by which you leave and return to the hotel. Be alert for persons watching your movements.

- Note whether hotel security locks up certain access points after dark. Plan to use the main entrance upon return to the property.

- Speak with the bellman, concierge, and front desk staff regarding safe areas around the city in which to jog, dine, or sightsee. Ask about local customs and which taxi companies to use or avoid.

- Do not take valuables to the spa or workout room.

- Be cautious when entering restrooms in the hotel. On occasion, unauthorized persons use these facilities to deal drugs or engage in prostitution or theft. Female travelers should be alert to placing purses on hangers on the inside of the lavatory doors or on the floor in stalls as these are two frequent locations for grab-and-run thefts.

- Purse snatchers and briefcase thieves are known to work hotel bars and restaurants, waiting for unknowing guests to drape these items on chairs or under tables only to discover them missing as they are departing. Keep items in view or "in touch." Be alert to scams involving an unknown person spilling a drink or food on your clothing. An accomplice may be preparing to steal your wallet, briefcase, or purse.

- The pool or beach area is a fertile area for thieves to take advantage of guests enjoying recreation. Leave valuables in the hotel room. Safeguard your room key and camera. Sign for food and beverages on your room bill rather than carrying cash.

- Prostitutes take advantage of travelers around the world through various ploys, use of "knock-out" drugs, and theft from the victim's room. Avoid engaging persons whom you do not know and refrain from inviting them to your guest room.

IN THE WORKPLACE

- The workplace, your home away from home: here you are safe and secure. It's the one place where you no longer have to worry about what you do or say. WRONG! You are probably safer here, but you should still take some precautions.

- Safeguard all sensitive or proprietary papers and documents. Do not leave them lying around in the office or on top of a desk.

- Guard your conversations. Do not allow unauthorized personnel to eavesdrop on discussions pertaining to proprietary information, personnel issues, or management planning or problems. In many countries, employees are debriefed by the local intelligence or security services in an effort to learn as much as possible about activities of American companies and their personnel.

- Be careful of all communications. Be aware that the monitoring of telephone calls, telegraph communications, and international mail is common in some countries.

TRAVELING BY TRAIN

In many countries, railroads continue to offer a safe, reliable, and comfortable means of travel between major metropolitan areas. Other countries, however, operate antiquated rail systems that are often overcrowded and seldom run on time. As a general rule, the more socially and economically advanced a country is, the more modern and reliable its rail service will be. Frequently, rail travel provides a more economical method of travel than other modes of transportation, and often it is the only available transportation to smaller cities and towns. But like any other means of transportation, rail travel can present some security risks.

Railroads are "soft" targets for several types of criminal or terrorist attacks. They operate over open ground and are easily accessible to the public. The tracks on which the trains operate are in the open for most of the distance they cover. This easy accessibility provides an inviting target for bombings and other forms of sabotage.

Railroad terminals and stations are like self-contained cities, open to the public for twenty-four hours a day. They provide a fertile ground for pickpockets, purse snatchers, baggage thieves, bombers, and other criminals to operate.

Trains themselves offer similar opportunities to criminals and terrorists. A train is like a hotel on wheels, offering temporary accommodations, such as restaurants, sleeping space, bars, and lounges. All of these can be, and often are, subject to criminal activities, including robbery, thievery, bombing, and even, albeit rarely, hostage-taking.

Some Precautionary Measures

Prior to departure:

- It should be noted that many cities have more than one railroad station. Travelers should confirm which station their train will depart from in advance. Make sure that you use the right one.

- Make reservations in advance to avoid long lines at rail station ticket counters. This is where pickpockets, baggage thieves, and purse snatchers like to operate. Your hotel concierge can assist in making reservations and picking up your ticket.

- Travel light and always keep your luggage under your control. In the time it takes to set down your luggage to check a timetable, a baggage thief can make off with it.

- Watch your tickets. Keep them in an inside pocket or purse to lessen the chance that they can be stolen.

- Do not discard your train ticket until you've completed your trip and have left the arrival area. In some countries you will be required to show your ticket at the station exit. If you do not have it, you may be required to purchase another one. Hold on to your ticket, whether or not a conductor checks it.

- Make certain that you board the right car and that it is going to your intended destination.

- If you have to transfer to another train to reach your destination, determine this in advance and know where you will make the transfer, the time of transfer, the train number, the departure time of your connecting train, and the track number if possible.

- Learn how to tell whether you are in the correct car and whether it goes to your destination. Name boards on the side of the car will tell you this.

For example, a name board might appear like this:

VENEZIA

Bologna–Firenze

ROMA

This shows that the car begins in Venice, stops in Bologna and Florence, and ends in Rome.

- Next to the steps leading into many train cars you should see the numeral "1" or "2," or both. The "1" indicates first class. The "2" indicates second class.

- Make certain you know how to spell and pronounce the name of your destination city so you recognize it when announced.

- Be alert to train splitting. This occurs when part of the train is split off and attached to another train while the remainder of the original train then continues on its way. Check with the ticket agent or onboard conductor to determine whether this applies to your itinerary. Find out in advance whether your car will have to be switched to another train en route, when and where this will occur, and the name of the stop just prior to the switching point. Prepare accordingly.

- Try not to schedule a late night or early morning arrival. You might find yourself stranded at a rail station with no public transportation.

- Whenever possible, arrange to be met by someone at your arrival point.

On Board the Train

- If possible, check unneeded luggage into the baggage car.

- Keep your unchecked luggage with you at all times. If you must leave your seat, either take your luggage with you or secure it to your seat or the baggage rack with a strong cable lock.

- Try to get a window seat. This provides a quick means of escape in the event of an accident.

- Have necessary international documents, including your passport, handy and ready for inspection by immigration officials at each border crossing.

- Keep your valuables with you at all times.

- If you have a private compartment, keep the door locked and identify anyone wishing to gain access. Know the names of your porters and ask them to identify themselves whenever entering your compartment.

- When in your compartment, be aware that some train thieves will spray chemicals inside to render the occupant unconscious, then enter and steal valuables. A locked door will at least keep them out.

- If you become suspicious of anyone, or someone bothers you, notify the conductor or other train personnel.

- If you must leave the train temporarily at a stop other than your destination, make certain that you are not left behind.

- An understanding of military time (the so-called twenty-four-hour clock) will make it easier for you to understand the train schedule.

- Make certain you have currency from each of the countries through which you will be traveling.

- On trains traveling through lesser-developed countries, it may be advisable to carry your own food and water.

Upon Arrival

- Make certain that you depart from the train at the correct location.

- Use only authorized taxis for transportation to your hotel or other destination.

- Be alert to criminals such as pickpockets, baggage thieves, and/or unauthorized taxi drivers/guides.

DRIVING ABROAD

- Obtain an International Drivers Permit (IDP). This can be purchased through your AAA Club. Have your passport photos and a completed application. There will be a fee involved. Carry both your IDP and your state driver's license with you at all times.

- Some countries have a minimum and maximum driving age. Check the laws before you drive in any country.

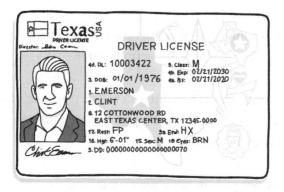

- Always "buckle up." Some countries have penalties for people who violate this law.

- If you rent a car, always purchase the liability insurance. If you do not, this could lead to financial disaster.

- Many countries have different driving rules. Study those rules before you begin driving in that country.

- If the drivers in the country you are visiting drive on the opposite side of the road than in the US, practice driving in a less populated area before attempting to drive in the heavy traffic.

- Be vigilant when driving through the countryside. Many countries require you to honk your horn before going around a sharp corner or to flash your lights before passing.

- Find out before you start your journey which lane has the right of way in a traffic circle.

- Always know the route you will be traveling. Have a copy of a good road map, and chart your course before beginning.

- Do not pick up hitchhikers or strangers.

- When entering or exiting your vehicle, be aware of your surroundings.

PERSONAL CONDUCT OVERSEAS

A hostile or even friendly intelligence organization is always on the lookout for sources vulnerable to coercion, addictions, greed, or emotional manipulation. To eliminate, or at least diminish, the possibility of doing something inadvertent that would bring your activities to the special attention of one of these agencies, here are some things to remember:

- DO NOT do anything which might be misconstrued or reflect poorly on your personal judgment or professional demeanor, or be embarrassing to you and/or your company.

- DO NOT gossip about character flaws, financial problems, emotional relationships, or marital difficulties of anyone working for the company, including you. This type of information is eagerly sought after by those who would like to exploit you or another employee.

- DO NOT carry, use, or purchase any narcotics, marijuana, or other abused drugs. Some countries have very stringent laws covering the import or use of medications and other substances. If you are using a prescribed medication that contains any narcotic substance or other medication that is subject to abuse, such as amphetamines or tranquilizers, carry a copy of the doctor's prescription for all medications and check your local restrictions and requirements prior to departure. Some countries may require additional documentation/certification from your doctor.

- DO NOT let a friendly ambience and alcohol over-ride your good sense and capacity when it comes to social drinking. In some countries, heavy drinking in the form of toasting is quite common, and very few Westerners can keep up with a local national when it comes to drinking the national brew. An intoxicated or hungover business negotiator could, if not careful, prove to be very embarrassing and expensive to the company. In these situations, prudence is essential.

- DO NOT engage in "black market" activities, such as the illegal exchange of currency or the purchase of religious icons or other local antiquities.

- DO NOT accept or deliver letters, packages, or anything else from anyone unknown to you. You have no way of knowing what you are carrying, and it could result in you being arrested for illegally exporting a prohibited item.

- DO NOT engage in any type of political or religious activity, or carry any political or religious tracts or brochures, or publications likely to be offensive in the host country, such as pornography or merce-nary/weapons.

- DO NOT photograph anything that appears to be associated with the military or internal security of the country, including airports, ports, or restricted areas, such as military installations. If in doubt, err on the side of caution.

- DO NOT purchase items that are illegal to import, such as endangered species or agricultural products.

I'VE BEEN ARRESTED!—WHAT DO I DO NOW?

Foreign police and intelligence agencies detain persons for myriad reasons or for no other reason than suspicion or curiosity. The best advice is to exercise good judgment and to remain professional in your demeanor. If you are detained or arrested for any reason, here are some points to remember:

- DO ask to contact the nearest embassy or consulate representing your country. As a citizen of another country, you have this right. But that does not mean that your hosts will allow you to exercise that right. If you are refused or just ignored, continue to make the request periodically until they accede and let you contact your embassy or consulate.

- DO stay calm, maintain your dignity, and do not do anything to provoke the arresting officer(s).

- DO NOT admit anything or volunteer any information.

- DO NOT sign anything. Often, part of the detention procedure is to ask or tell the detainee to sign a written report. Decline politely until such time as the document is examined by an attorney or an embassy/consulate representative.

- DO NOT accept anyone on face value. When the representative from the embassy or consulate arrives, request some identification before discussing your situation.

- DO NOT fall for the ruse of helping the ones who are detaining you in return for your release. They can be very imaginative in their proposals on how you can be of assistance to them. Do not agree to anything. If they will not take no for an answer, do not make a firm commitment or sign anything. Tell them that you will think it over and let them know. Once out of their hands, contact the affiliate or your embassy for protection and assistance in getting out of the country.

IF YOU ARE THE VICTIM OF A CRIME OVERSEAS

- Contact the nearest US embassy, consulate, or consular agency for assistance.

- Contact local police to report the incident and obtain immediate help with safety concerns. Request a copy of the police report.

- Consular personnel can provide assistance to crime victims. When a US citizen becomes the victim of a crime overseas, he or she may suffer physical, emotional, or financial injuries. Additionally, the emotional impact of the crime may be intensified because the victim is in unfamiliar surroundings. The victim may not be near sources of comfort and support, fluent in the local language, or knowledge-able about local laws and customs.

- Consuls, consular agents, and local employees at overseas posts are familiar with local government agencies and resources in the country where they work. They can help American crime victims with issues such as:

  * Replacing a stolen passport

  * Contacting family, friends, or employers

  * Obtaining appropriate medical care

  * Addressing emergency needs that arise as a result of the crime

* Obtaining general information about the local criminal justice process and information about your case

* Obtaining information about local resources to assist victims, including foreign crime victim compensation programs

* Obtaining information about US crime victim assistance and compensation programs

* Obtaining a list of local attorneys who speak English

- Consular officials cannot, however, investigate crimes, provide legal advice, or represent you in court, serve as official interpreters or translators, or pay legal, medical, or other fees for you.

HELP FOR AMERICANS OVERSEAS

The Bureau of Consular Affairs, Overseas Citizens Services, is committed to assisting American citizens who become victims of crime while traveling, working, or residing abroad. Government officials, known as consuls or consular officers, are posted at embassies and consulates in nearly 250 cities throughout the world. They are responsible for assisting US citizens who may be traveling, working, or residing abroad. In addition, in approximately fifty cities where a significant number of Americans reside or visit and there is no US embassy or consulate, consular agents provide emergency assistance to US citizens. Consuls, consular agents, and local employees work with their counterparts in the Bureau of Consular Affairs Overseas Citizens Services Office in Washington, DC, to provide emergency and non-emergency services to Americans abroad.

How to Contact

Consular duty personnel are available for emergency assistance twenty-four hours a day, seven days a week, at embassies, consulates, and consular agencies overseas and in Washington, DC. To contact the Office of Overseas Citizens Services in the US, call 1-888-407-4747 (during business hours) or 202-647-5225 (after hours). Outside the US, call 1-202-501-4444. Contact information for US embassies, consulates, and consular agencies overseas is on the internet.

INDIVIDUAL REACTIONS TO CRIME VICTIMIZATION

How a person reacts to being the victim of a crime varies based on several factors, including how they typically handle stress, the nature and duration of the crime, their physical safety during the crime, and the number and type of support systems available. Reactions to a crime may be immediate or delayed. The physical, emotional, or cognitive symptoms a person may experience could include nausea, headaches, fatigue, hyperventilation, or sleeping problems. Some people report feelings of anxiety or fear, hypervigilance, guilt, anger, or isolation. Some experience difficulty making decisions, short-term memory problems, difficulty concentrating, or recurring memories of the crime.

It is important to realize that these are normal feelings, behaviors, and reactions to an abnormal event. One of the first things to pay attention to is your need to feel safer. Addressing safety concerns and receiving emotional support can help. For most people, the reactions described above diminish with time. If these reactions persist, are disrupting your life, or are getting worse after three or four weeks, you should consider seeking professional assistance.

Resources and Information for Crime Victims

Victim Assistance. If you are the victim of a crime while overseas, you may benefit from specialized resources for crime victims available in the US. Throughout the United States, thousands of local crime victim assistance programs offer help to victims of violent crime. Most will also help residents of their community who have been the victim of a crime in another country. These include rape crisis counseling programs, shelter and counseling programs for battered women, support groups and bereavement counseling for family members of homicide victims, diagnostic and treatment programs for child abuse victims, assistance for victims of drunk-driving crashes, and others.

Victim Compensation. All states operate crime-victim compensation programs and nearly half of them offer benefits to their residents who are victims of violent crime overseas. These state compensation programs provide financial assistance to eligible victims for reimbursement of expenses, such as medical treatment, counseling, funeral costs, lost income, loss of support, and others. Generally, victim compensation programs require the victim to report the crime to law enforcement. They usually request a copy of the police report.

"There are no foreign lands. It is the traveler only who is foreign."

—ROBERT LOUIS STEVENSON

CHAPTER 7 REVIEW

PRACTICE ASSIGNMENT— TRAVEL PREPARATION AND PLANNING

HOW WELL DID YOU PREPARE?

THIS CHAPTER HAS EXPLORED THE WAYS YOU SHOULD PLAN AND PREPARE before you begin your trip. It also discusses the details of travel—the ins and outs of hotels, transportation, and more. Finally, you learned about what to do if you are unfortunate enough to be mistakenly put in jail in a foreign country and what resources are available for victims of crimes overseas.

Now, let's put some of that knowledge to work with a practice scenario.

PRACTICAL EXAMPLE

- Semi-permissive environment (area with some government control)

- Traveling for business and encountering a series of unfortunate events

You've finished up a meeting in Shanghai and your business associate recommends you enjoy the countryside in China. He suggests you take a train to your next meeting in Beijing. So, you purchase a ticket for a soft sleeper, which includes a comfy four-berth area with two sofa beds and a table. There is a locking door, which you like a lot. You are a little confused going through the security check, but everything seems in order and you board the train. You aren't sure about how to check luggage, so you decide to haul your two suitcases in with you. You settle in and start to work on your laptop. But then someone else comes into the compartment. The people seem okay, and you gesture and establish a friendly rapport.

Everything goes along well until the conductor comes in to check tickets. Where did you place your ticket? You can't find it. You try to explain, but the language barrier is a problem. The conductor is not happy. There is an interim stop. You are taken off the train and are still trying to explain what has happened. You offer to pay, but by this time, the train has departed. You look around. During the confusion, you were distracted, and your briefcase is missing. Now you are panicked. Your brief-case contained your passport and most of your funds. You alert an attendant, but he shrugs, not understanding. You start to get really upset. This upsets the attendant, who feels threatened. Suddenly, a uniformed officer is on the scene. You feel relieved, but this feeling only lasts a second because now you are being arrested.

STUDY GUIDE QUESTIONS

What should you do next to mitigate your arrest?

What could you have done to prevent this situation from happening in the first place?

STUDY GUIDE ANSWERS

What should you do next to mitigate your arrest?

First, ask to contact the nearest embassy or consulate repre-senting your country. If you are refused or just ignored, continue to make the request.

Remain calm, maintain your dignity, and do not do anything to provoke the arresting officer. Do not admit anything or volunteer any information.

The officer in charge asks you to sign something. You can't read it since it is written in Chinese. You politely decline, knowing that part of the detention procedure is to ask or tell the detainee to sign a written report. You state that you will wait until the document can be examined by an attorney or an embassy/consulate representative.

Someone finally comes in saying they are from the US Embassy. You ask for identification, which is provided. You proceed to explain that your passport was stolen along with your briefcase.

What could you have done to prevent this situation from happening in the first place?

Unfortunately, you didn't retain your ticket for the train, and this led to your being inattentive, and then your briefcase was stolen. Inattention was the cause of all this misery. The embassy representative is able to explain your situation and you are soon sprung from this unfortunate situation.

NOTES:

_____

_____

_____

_____

_____

_____

_____

_____

_____

_____

_____

_____

_____

_____

_____

_____

_____

_____

NOTES

GLOSSARY OF TERMS

"The world is a book and those who do not travel read only one page."

—ST. AUGUSTINE

Agencies. Intelligence and law enforcement agencies are government agencies devoted to collecting information related to host government security and defense. These agencies can collect information on travelers, including obtaining proprietary corporate information.

Alert Mode. Alert Mode is one of the stages in the Modes of Awareness cycle. It is the constant observation of the environment and scanning for potential threats. A person should be in Alert Mode at all times. Time in Alert Mode may last days, weeks, or months. Transition from Alert to Pre-Crisis Mode is triggered when potential threats are recognized. To prevent stalled decisions and actions, invisible thresholds are set, and the OODA loop is used to help make decisions.

Body language. Nonverbal physical movements and expressions communicate intentional or unintentional thoughts and emotions. A simple, yet powerful, body language signal is when a person crosses his or her arms. Other than indicating that a person is physically cold, this typically indicates an unconscious barrier has been raised.

COMSEC. A process by which a group or individual can deny adversaries information about intentions by identifying, controlling, and protecting evidence of the planning and execution of travel.

Crisis Mode. Crisis Mode is one of the Modes of Awareness stages. It is the tactical action against the threat in order to dominate, elude, or escape the threat. This is not the time for decision-making. That process should have been completed in Pre-Crisis Mode. Crisis Mode is triggered by the breach of the invisible threshold. Crisis Mode may last seconds or minutes. Transitioning back to Pre-Crisis Mode should occur sooner rather than later. Increased exposure to the threat may decrease survivability. Threat domination, elusion, or escape triggers transition back to Pre-Crisis Mode.

Cultural Awareness (CA). This is the assessment and understanding of a specific geographic location's culture, including cultural-specific aspects, such as social protocol, etiquette, mannerisms, gestures, and other Personal Awareness traits. Cultural Awareness coupled with Personal Awareness can help decrease Third-Party Awareness and help you navigate through possible threats undetected.

Daisy chain. This type of surveillance can be used instead of a floating box to decrease possible compromise of the operation. A daisy chain is a passive, static, multimember, linear surveillance where individual surveillants are staged along the known route of a target person. The surveillants are typically ahead of the target person, observing and reporting the target's arrival and departure at specific locations along the target's route.

Demeanor (actions). The image you convey is defined as your physical actions, which include gestures, manners, language, handshake, walk, talk, and other things that the general public can observe. Chapter 4 is dedicated to country-specific culture projection and demeanor traits for you to use during travel.

Economic espionage. (1) Whoever knowingly performs targeting or acquisition of trade secrets to (2) knowingly benefit any foreign government, foreign instrumentality, or foreign agent. (Title 18 U.S.C., Section 1831.)

Environmental threats. Environmental threats include natural disasters and threats like hurricanes, tsunamis, winter storms, volcano eruptions, and mudslides. You need to learn what hazards are common in the area you will be visiting and how to handle challenges if they should arise.

First-line gear (difficult to change). As it relates to Projection, this is your birthday suit. You want to identify any characteristics that are culturally offensive, make you stand out in a crowd, or make you a threat.

Floating box. Once the target moves from location to location, this type of surveillance may be used. A floating box is defined as a multimember, mobile surveillance box that discreetly surrounds the target person during foot or mobile movement. Each member rotates in and out of position to maintain constant observation. This is very difficult for a team to perfect and employ. Risk of compromise is high using this tactic.

Foreign agent. Any officer, employee, proxy, servant, delegate, or representative of a foreign government.

Foreign instrumentality. (1) Any agency, bureau, ministry, component, institution, or association; (2) any legal, commercial, or business organization, corporation, firm, or entity; that is (3) substantially owned, controlled, sponsored, commanded, managed, or dominated by a foreign government.

Health threats. Health threats consist of, but are not limited to, viruses, bacteria, chemicals, and other harmful substances spread human-to-human, airborne-to-human, water- or food-to-human, and vector-to-human. It's important to know what health threats are common in the area you plan to visit and prepare before your trip.

Intrusion detection. Discreet techniques and tactics that can be used to determine surveillance status.

Nonpermissive environment (No US policy exists). A nonpermissive environment, sometimes called a denied area, is an area where there is little or no government. Control is induced through hostile actions of non-government forces. Support of the United States or its citizens is minimal. Country example: Syria.

OODA loop. This four-step process helps with decision-making. The steps are Observation, Orientation, Decision, and Action.

Permissive environment (US policy exists). A permissive environment is an area under complete control by the government. The government is supported 100 percent by its citizens. The most important part: the host government and its citizens support the United States. Utopia, if you will, where everyone lives in harmony. Not sure a permissive environment truly exists. Canada maybe?

Personal Awareness (PA). The image and demeanor you project to blend in within a specific culture, reduce threat vulnerabilities, and reduce Third-Party Awareness. Personal

Awareness ensures an individual assesses and manages specific character traits that separate him or her from the intended culture of interest. Personal Awareness is also the ability to recognize and identify your physical characteristics and the actions that personify your individual projection and demeanor.

Physical surveillance. When an individual or group of individuals physically follow, observe, or track a target's every movement.

Pre-Crisis Mode. One of the Modes of Awareness stages. Pre-Crisis Mode is the constant observation of the identified potential threats. Time in Pre-Crisis Mode may last hours or days. Pre-Crisis Mode is triggered by the identification of a potential threat. This mode allows a person to determine courses of action and designate an invisible threshold that activates Crisis Mode. All decisions made in this mode prepare you to transition to Crisis Mode for action. When the threat breaches the invisible threshold, Crisis Mode is initiated. To prevent stalled decisions and actions, invisible thresholds are set, and the OODA loop is used to make decisions.

Projection (appearance). This is your physical appearance, what the general public can observe, and includes clothing, jewelry, technology, grooming standards, gender, race, and accessories.

Protocol. International rules and social behavior, such as body language and communication, in accordance with a specific culture. Protocol includes meetings, greetings, manners, and other actions within a culture.

Raids/robbery threats. An organized assault conducted by criminals or terrorists. By definition a criminal is a person guilty of a crime or crimes. Criminals commit theft, rape, murder, and everything in between. The most significant raids to highlight are carjacking, kidnappings, and hostage situations.

Second-line gear (easy to change). As it relates to Projection, encompasses anything that touches your skin. Second-line gear includes things like hats, sunglasses, shirts, pants, underwear, socks, gloves, necklaces, bracelets, watches, and rings. These items make up a large part of the traits that define a person and are used to separate them from others.

Semi-permissive environment (US policy may exist). A semi-permissive environment has a government that yields questionable control. The citizens may or may not support the government. The government and citizens may or may not support the United States. Corruption is usually the wolf for these countries. Country example: Philippines. Most of the world is semi-permissive.

Setting the box. Most surveillance teams "pick up" a target from a static location like home or work. To "set the box" is defined as multimember, static surveillance covering all four sides of a structure. Each position assigned is in direct relation to possible exit and entrance points used by the target person. The idea is that one of the team members will observe the target person departing or entering the structure and report a positive identification, location, dress, and activity to the rest of the team.

Situational Awareness (SA). This is a conscious and constant focus on the environment to detect, validate, and confirm threats. Detection is triggered by both instinct and observation.

Surveillance. This is an assessment of vulnerabilities in an attempt to determine any information available from any source about you or your activities, such as lifestyle or behavior that can be used against you (pattern of life).

Technical surveillance. This type of monitoring consists of following, observing, and tracking a target with electronic equipment.

Technological threats. Technological threats include audio collection devices, video collection devices, tracking devices, cell phone exploitation, and laptop exploitation used to collect information illegally. It's important to understand what threat each poses and what defenses and actions can be taken.

TEDD. This acronym stands for Time, Environment, Distance, and Demeanor. If you see someone repeatedly over time, in different environments, and over distance, or one who displays poor demeanor, then you can assume you're under surveillance.

Terrorism. A person or group using unlawful acts of violence to influence, coerce, or strike fear into people for ideological, political, or religious gains. Currently, there is not an internationally agreed definition of terrorism. You should research and learn about terrorist facts, groups, and tactics related to the area you plan to visit.

Third-line gear (remains through change). As it relates to Projection, this covers anything that touches your clothes. Third-line gear includes items like jackets, shoes, belts, man bags, purses, backpacks, wallets, passports, mobile phone, and laptops. These are items that people use for long periods of time (longevity items) or have in limited quantities when traveling.

THREAT. This acronym is a risk-assessment tool used to define technical, health, raid, environmental, agency, and terror threats in a specific geographical location. Using this acronym will help you assess and research potential threats, which will sensitize your senses, prep your Situational and Personal Awareness, and decrease your vulnerabilities.

Third-Party Awareness (3PA). This is the general public's perception of you and your actions. In a nutshell, when you feel like everyone is staring at you, they probably are. Third-Party Awareness includes citizens, law enforcement, criminals, and terrorists residing in the host country. To reduce Third-Party Awareness, you need to blend into the environment by using Personal Awareness (culturally driven projection and demeanor management) and Situational Awareness skillsets.

The Total Awareness System (TA). This holistic risk-assessment system reduces threat vulnerabilities through Situational, Personal, Cultural, and Third-Party Awareness. The Total Awareness System includes pre-deployment threat assessments, cultural assessments to blend in, heightened awareness, and identifying and escaping threats.

Trade secrets. All forms and types of financial, business, scientific, technical, economic, or engineering information, including patterns, plans, compilations, program devices, formulas, designs, prototypes, methods, techniques, processes, procedures, programs, or codes—whether tangible or intangible, and whether they are stored, compiled, or memorialized physically, electronically, graphically, photographically, or in writing—which the owner has taken reasonable measures to protect, and which have an independent economic value. Trade secrets are commonly called classified proprietary information, economic policy information, trade information, proprietary technology, or critical technology.

Theft of trade secrets occurs when someone: (1) knowingly performs targeting or acquisition of trade secrets, or intends to convert a trade secret; to (2) knowingly benefit anyone other than the owner. This is commonly referred to as ***industrial espionage***. (Title 18 U.S.C., Section 1832.)

"Not all those who wander are lost."

–J.R.R. TOLKIEN

REFERENCES

CHAPTER 2

Agan, R.D. "Intuitive Knowing as a Dimension of Nursing." *Advances in Nursing Science* 10, no. 1 (October 1987): 63–70. https://doi.org/10.1097/00012272-198710000-00011.

Brockmann, Erich N. and Willian P. Anthony. "The Influence of Tacit Knowledge and Collective Mind on Strategic Planning." *Journal of Managerial Issues* 10, no. 2 (Summer 1998): 204–22. https://www.jstor.org/stable/40604193.

Cannon-Bowers, Janis A., Eduardo Salas, and John S. Pruitt. "Establishing the Boundaries of a Paradigm for Decision-Making Research." *Human Factors: The Journal of the Human Factors and Ergonomics Society* 38, no. 2 (June 1, 1996): 193–203. https://doi.org/10.1177/001872089606380202.

Cohen, Marcin S. "The Naturalistic Basis of Decision Biases." In *Decision Making in Action: Models and Methods,* by Gary A. Klein, Judith Orasanu, and Robert Caldenwood, 50–99. Norwood, NJ: Ablex, 1993.

de Becker, Gavin. *The Gift of Fear.* New York: Dell Publishing, 1997.

Grossman, Dave and Loren Christensen. *On Combat: The Psychology and Physiology of Deadly Conflict in War and in Peace.* Colombia, Illinois: PPCT Research Publications, 2004. "On Sheep, Wolves, and Sheepdogs."

Klein, Gary A. "The Recognition-Primed Decision (RPD) Model: Looking Back, Looking Forward." In *Naturalistic Decision-Making* by Caroline Zsambok and Gary A. Klein, 285–292. Mahwah, NJ: Lawrence Erlbaum Associates, Inc., 1997. https://psycnet.apa.org/record/1997-97363-026.

Klein, Gary A., Roberta Calderwood, and Donald MacGregor. "Critical Decision Method for Eliciting Knowledge." *IEEE Transactions on Systems, Man, and Cybernetics* 19, no. 3 (May/June 1989): 462–72. https://doi.org/10.1109/21.31053.

Polanyi, Michael. *Personal Knowledge: Towards a Post-Critical Philosophy.* Chicago: The University of Chicago Press, 1958.

Randel, Josephine M., H. Lauren Pugh, and Stephen K. Reed. "Differences in Expert and Novice Situation Awareness in Naturalistic Decision-Making." *International Journal of Human-Computer Studies* 45, no. 5 (November 1996): 579–97. https://doi.org/10.1006/ijhc.1996.0068.

Schon, Donald A. *The Reflective Practitioner: How Professionals Think in Action*. New York City: Basic Books, 1984.

Smithson, Michael. *Ignorance and Uncertainty: Emerging Paradigms*. New York City: Springer Verlag, 1989.

Sternberg, Robert J. and Joseph A. Horvath. *Tacit Knowledge in Professional Practice: Researcher and Practitioner Perspectives*. Mahwah, NJ: Lawrence Erlbaum Associates, Inc., 1999.

Uttaro, Michael T. "Naturalistic Decision-Making in Law Enforcement Practice: Exploring the Process." PhD diss., Virginia Polytechnic Institute and State University, 2002.

CHAPTER 3

Bosrock, Mary Murray. *Asian Business Customs & Manners: A Country-by-Country Guide*. Minnetonka, MN: Meadowbrook Press, 2007.

Eyring, Pamela. The Protocol School of Washington Curriculum. Washington, DC, 2008.

Irwin, Will. *The Jedburghs: The Secret History of the Allied Special Forces, France 1944.* New York City: Public Affairs/Perseus Book Group, 2005.

CHAPTER 4

Burton, Fred and Scott Stewart. "Threats, Situational Awareness and Perspective." Risk Assistance Network and Exchange, August 22, 2007. https://worldview.stratfor.com/article/threats-situational-awareness-and-perspective.

The CIA World Factbook, www.cia.gov.

Communicaid, http://www.communicaid.com/.

Eyring, Pamela. The Protocol School of Washington Curriculum. Washington, DC, 2008.

CHAPTER 5

ACM IV Security Services. *Surveillance Countermeasures: A Serious Guide to Detecting, Evading, and Eluding Threats to Personal Privacy.* Boulder: Paladin Press, 1994.

Ball, Kirstie, David Lyon, David Maurakami Wood, Clive Norris, and Charles Raab. "A Report on the Surveillance Society: For the Information Commissioner by the Surveillance Studies Network." September 2006. https:// ico.org.uk/media/about-the-ico/documents/1042390/ surveillance-society-full-report-2006.pdf.

Burton, Fred and Scott Stewart. "Threats, Situational Awareness and Perspective." Risk Assistance Network and Exchange, August 22, 2007. https://worldview.stratfor. com/article/threats-situational-awareness-and-perspective.

McCullagh, Declan. "RFID Tags: Big Brother in Small Packages." *CNET News*, January 13, 2003. https://www.cnet. com/news/rfid-tags-big-brother-in-small-packages/.

Vlahos, James. "Surveillance Society: New High-Tech Cameras Are Watching You." *Popular Mechanics*, October 1, 2009. https://www.popularmechanics.com/military/a2398/4236865/.

CHAPTER 6

Business Travel Abroad. Department of State, Overseas Security Council, Diplomatic Publications, Released 1994.

Burton, Fred and Scott Stewart. "Threats, Situational Awareness and Perspective." Risk Assistance Network and Exchange, August 22, 2007. https://worldview.stratfor.com/article/threats-situational-awareness-and-perspective.

"Denmark Investigates Botulism Outbreak." Food Safety News, March 16, 2021. https://www.foodsafetynews.com/2021/03/denmark-investigates-botulism-outbreak/.

The National Fire Protection Association, http://www.nfpa.org/.

OnGuardOnline, http://www.onguardonline.gov/.

The Red Cross, http://www.redcross.org/.

World Health Organization, www.who.int.

CHAPTER 7

American Automobile Association, http://www.aaa.com/.

Burton, Fred and Scott Stewart. "Threats, Situational Awareness and Perspective." Risk Assistance Network and Exchange, August 22, 2007. https://worldview.stratfor.com/article/threats-situational-awareness-and-perspective.

References

Business Travel Abroad. Department of State, Overseas Security Council, Diplomatic Publications, Released 1994.

Carjacking: Don't be a Victim. Overseas Security Advisory Council, Department of State, OSAC Publication 2005.

Centers for Disease Control and Prevention, Division of Global Migration and Quarantine, National Center for Preparedness, Detection, and Control of Infectious Diseases, Atlanta GA, 2009.

Counterterrorism. The National Counterterrorism Center, Counterterrorism Calendar, September 2008.

ABOUT THE AUTHOR

CLINT IS A RETIRED NAVY SEAL WITH MORE THAN TWENTY YEARS OF service. He continues to serve by empowering good people with safety and security skills at home, work and abroad. His services have helped Fortune 500 companies, politicians, celebrities, and more. He's the bestselling author of *100 Deadly Skills*, as well as *100 Deadly Skills: Survival Edition, 100 Deadly Skills: Combat Edition,* and *The Rugged Life.*

Made in the USA
Monee, IL
19 February 2024

53657928R00184